Empire Style

Authentic Decor

BERNARD CHEVALLIER
MARC WALTER

with 220 colour illustrations

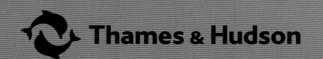
Thames & Hudson

Contents

Introduction

The lavish lifestyle of the French aristocracy and its accompanying arts, rudely interrupted by the fall of the monarchy in summer 1792, made a tentative reappearance after the death of Robespierre two years later before experiencing a true renaissance under the government of the Directoire. It continued to flourish during the Consulate, and once Napoleon had declared himself Emperor, he never ceased in his quest to make Paris into the showcase of the civilized world. There was no member of the imperial family, no *maréchal* of the Empire, no *bourgeois gentilhomme* who did not aspire to live in one of the great houses left abandoned by the flight of their former owners. These *nouveaux riches* invented a new way of living, and they entrusted its architectural setting to such talented men as Percier, Fontaine and Berthault. Their designs were to introduce into these older buildings the even more ancient styles of Greece, Rome and Egypt.

While the decor changed, the functions of a fine home remained the same. Society life still demanded salons where visitors could be received, music could be heard, and billiards could be played. Ideally, they would be on the ground floor, so that people could enjoy the garden as well. On the first floor, the mistress of the house had her own apartments, separate from those of her husband. These apartments were decorated in differing styles – more solemn and dignified for Monsieur, more elegant and refined for Madame. Personal hygiene was becoming a greater concern, and larger houses were often equipped with bathrooms. As far as heating was concerned, the old stoves were gradually being replaced by new underfloor systems, and lighting was also greatly improved through refinements in the design of oil lamps.

In short, everyone who found grace and favour with the Emperor was expected to submit to his will and support the makers of luxury goods – especially the silkworkers of Lyons and the porcelain and glass factories, not to mention all the craftspeople connected with the world of fashion.

As the Emperor himself commented when in exile on St Helena, the Revolution, despite all its horrors, had been the true cause of this revival of luxurious living, and the fifteen years of his rule opened the way to the triumph of the bourgeoisie during the 19th century.

Right: A porcelain table-top, made in a single piece by the Sèvres factory for Josephine Bonaparte, illustrated in the *Recueil de decorations intérieures* published by Percier and Fontaine in 1801. The central medallion depicts the love of Paris and Helen; it is surrounded by motifs inspired by antiquity.

Opposite: The ballroom in the palace of Compiègne was commissioned by Napoleon in 1809 and completed in 1813. During the Second Empire it was embellished with two statues. This one, representing Madame Mère, the mother of Napoleon, is a copy made in Carrara

of the original statue by Antonio Canova (1757–1822) at Chatsworth House in England. It belonged to Elisa, Napoleon's sister.

Overleaf: A portrait of the diplomat Antoine-René-Charles-Mathurin de Laforest (1756–1846), painted by François-André Vincent in 1804. He is shown in a fashionable interior with his wife, née Catherine-Marie Le Cuillier de Beaumanoir and daughter Marie-Caroline-Antoinette. Above his desk is a clock decorated with an allegorical figure of Study, similar to one delivered to Fontainebleau in 1806.

Houses

While public architecture enjoyed a great revival under Napoleon, private architecture was limited mainly to *maisons de rapport* (apartment buildings), since the late 18th century had already provided the capital with an abundance of fine houses that were still in excellent condition. Architects therefore tended to work predominantly on interiors, updating them in accordance with the tastes and comforts of the day. Some, like Louis-Martin Berthault, became true virtuosos of interior decoration, as recalled by the Duchesse d'Abrantès: 'Berthault had taste, and it was exquisite taste; I have never seen any apartment designed by him that was other than very fine. That of Mme Récamier was one of the best and most refined; the dining room, the bedroom, the first salon, the main salon, everything was magnificent, and elegantly furnished. The bedroom, indeed, served as a model for everything else of its kind: I do not think anyone has ever bettered it.'

The layout of rooms was virtually identical in both private houses and grand châteaux. Usually one entered through a hall that could also serve as an anteroom. Its design was always relatively simple, the floor typically paved with octagonal slabs of pale limestone punctuated by black stone, while the walls might be of fine ashlar, plastered, or in more modest interiors covered with wallpaper. Its furnishings were always simple: a stove, a lantern, and some benches, and stools of painted wood covered with wool velvet, on which the footmen would sit awaiting their master's orders. The usher sat at a small desk of dark-stained wood, writing down the names of visitors. The anteroom gave access to the reception rooms, and often to the staircase leading to the upper floors. From it one entered the dining room, usually decorated with elegant simplicity, and this led in turn to the reception rooms: salon, music room, billiard room, and – the *pièce de résistance* in the homes of the truly wealthy – the gallery, where collectors could exhibit their finest paintings, sculptures and *objets d'art*. Joachim Murat, Grand Duke of Berg and future King of Naples, had one built in the Château de Villiers, near Paris, to display the antiquities he had brought back from Italy, and Josephine commissioned Berthault to build a large top-lit gallery which was so majestically proportioned that it aroused the admiration of Napoleon himself. Beyond the reception rooms, and often upstairs, was the private apartment, sometimes also preceded by an anteroom; this would consist of a study, a boudoir for Madame, a library for Monsieur, bathing and dressing facilities, and above all a magnificent bedroom that was treated like a reception room, and richly furnished in a manner commensurate with the wealth of the proprietor. The decor and furnishings at this time were based on a rather unusual mixture of styles

Left: After the Revolution, building soon resumed in Paris. This is the garden elevation of a new house built in 1799 for himself by the architect Ollivier, in the rue Pépinière in the Faubourg Saint-Honoré.

Opposite: What is now the Hôtel Bourrienne in Paris was bought in 1801 by Bonaparte's private secretary, Louis-Antoine Fauvelet de Bourrienne, who engaged the architect Etienne-Chérubin Leconte, and it seems that the interior decoration is due to him. The three main rooms on the ground floor, opening out to the garden, are the bedroom, salon and dining room. With Malmaison, this interior is the finest example of the style of the early 1800s, imbued with late 18th-century elegance.

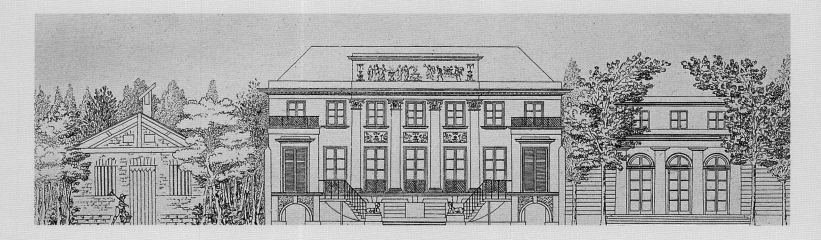

inspired for the most part by the classical world. But not all homes went to the extremes denounced by the anonymous author of *Quelques semaines à Paris* (A Few Weeks in Paris), who railed against houses that boasted an 'Italian marble staircase, French anteroom, Egyptian bed, Greek armchairs, Prussian fireplace, Etruscan candlesticks, Japanese vases and Roman drapes'; generally, the impression would be one of serious or even restrained grandeur, reflecting the talent and imagination of the designer.

In Paris, kitchens were usually situated below ground, whereas in the country they might be in a separate building. Spaces were provided for the meat store, the *rôtisserie*, the *patisserie*, the pantry, the washhouse and the servants' dining room. Stables, coachhouses, and lodgings for the coachmen, grooms and housekeeper would also be in the outbuildings. Horses were the only means of transport, and so the stables had an important role to play. At Malmaison, at the time of Josephine's death, the stables contained twenty-five horses (six of them mares), and the coachhouses no fewer than twenty-three vehicles for different purposes – coaches, cabriolets, chaises, phaetons and barouches.

In some of the larger private houses, there was also a chapel, sometimes situated in the area of the service rooms, as at King Louis Napoleon's townhouse in the rue Cerutti,

and at Malmaison, where it was in the outbuildings adjoining the music room. More often than not, the liturgical requisites were stored in a cupboard that was opened only just before the service. After re-establishing the Catholic faith, Napoleon took it upon himself to set an example by making sure that each of his imperial palaces had a chapel. While several already had one – Saint-Cloud, Fontainebleau, and Strasbourg, where it was simply relocated – Napoleon was quick to build one in those that didn't. In the Tuileries, the narrowness of the building unfortunately made it impossible for Fontaine to design a chapel of suitable dimensions. At Compiègne, Berthault had much more freedom, as the chapel was built *de novo* in an inner court of the palace; at Rambouillet, a simple oratory for Marie-Louise was installed in one of the towers of the old feudal residence.

In addition to chapels, Napoleon equipped his residences with theatres – an indispensable feature of court life. Fontainebleau and the Trianon at Versailles already had theirs, but he commissioned Fontaine to build one at Saint-Cloud. It was inaugurated in 1803, and had five hundred seats distributed over three tiers. Fontaine built the Tuileries theatre on the site of the old Salle de la Convention; it held as many as 1,200 people, took a year and a half to construct, and was opened in January 1808. It was rare,

Previous pages: The courtyard of the Hôtel Bourrienne. The building had been begun in 1787; Bourrienne bought it in 1801 and entrusted alterations to the architect Leconte. The house originally opened out to the street through a porch, but in 1828 that was replaced by a new wing. The courtyard façade, with a little flight of steps on the left, has remained untouched, and still bears four allegorical figures of Fame, attributed to the sculptor François-Frédéric Lemot.

Right: The Hôtel Bourrienne is still a private house, and it retains its charm despite the changes it has undergone.

however, for private homes to incorporate theatres: there were virtually none in Paris simply through lack of space, but a few country houses did have them. One in the château of Saint-Leu, home of King Louis Napoleon and Queen Hortense, held between three and four hundred spectators; there was one at Malmaison, hastily built by Fontaine in 1802, with two or three hundred seats. Generally, though, people made do with small, portable stages that could easily be assembled in the largest room in the house. This was also the case at Malmaison before it had its permanent theatre: a portable stage was erected initially in the music room and then moved to the great hall on the second floor.

These luxuries remained unusual, though, because most Parisians lived in houses whose different floors accommodated people from different social classes. In his *Lettres d'un mameluck* (*Letters of a Mameluke, or a Moral and Critical Picture of the Manners of Paris*), published in 1803, Joseph Lavallée wrote: 'Shopkeepers occupy the lower part; rich people, the first floor; persons in easy circumstances, the second; people in office, the third; working men, the fourth; and the distressed part of the community, the higher storeys.' This lack of privacy came as a shock to foreigners, as the novelist Maria Edgeworth wrote in the same year: 'You know the Parisian houses are inhabited by hordes of different people, and the stairs are in fact streets, and dirty streets, to their dwellings.' The apartments were laid out with very little concern for comfort and hygiene: bathrooms were rare, and lavatories practically non-existent. The German composer Johann Friedrich Reichardt, who travelled to Paris in 1798, reported that 'there are none at all; in other houses where I lived, they were dreadful places where no man of any sensitivity would wish to venture.'

Above: The garden front of the château of Malmaison, shown in a painting by Auguste Garnerey as it looked after Berthault had partially masked it with rich vegetation that almost completely concealed the ground floor. The striped canopy of the pavilion and the two red marble obelisks can only just be seen.

THESE PAGES
Left: Château Margaux, the archetypal neoclassical country house in the region of Bordeaux, was built in 1810–16 for the luxury-loving Marquis de la Colonilla, a Spaniard who had made his fortune in Cuba. He entrusted the commission to Louis Combes (1757–1818), the leading architect in Bordeaux, who had designed numerous buildings in and around the city. The château was built on a rectangular plan on four levels. The entrance front is marked by a portico consisting of four huge Ionic columns surmounted by a triangular pediment empty of sculpture. The garden front is simpler, with four Ionic pilasters. The vineyard of Château Margaux, of which the wine was classified as *premier grand cru* as long ago as 1855, is one of the most celebrated in the Médoc region.

Opposite: Looking from the dining room at Malmaison towards a monumental bust of Napoleon in the main stairwell. It is a replica, made in Carrara, of the head of the statue of Napoleon as Mars the Peacemaker by Canova, the original of which stands in Apsley House, the London residence of the Duke of Wellington. The decoration of the dining room, markedly influenced by the wall paintings of Pompeii, features eight dancers painted on stucco by Louis Lafitte (1770–1828), after drawings by Percier. Further references to the art of Antiquity include thyrsus motifs painted on the pilasters in the rotunda.

PREVIOUS PAGES

Pages 18–19: The draughtsman's instruments and drawings by Charles Percier (1764–1838) are a reminder of the key role played by Percier and Pierre-François-Léonard Fontaine (1762–1853) in the spread of neoclassical architecture throughout Europe. Their dedication and speed of execution won them the trust of the Emperor, who generally had little confidence in the profession. Their prodigious talents spread to all fields, and their legendary friendship earned them the nickname of the 'Dioscuri' (the twins Castor and Pollux, in classical legend). They worked together so closely that it was impossible to tell who had designed what.

Pages 20–21: Percier and Fontaine, both pupils of the architect Peyre, began their careers at Malmaison, which Josephine acquired in April 1799 while Napoleon was in Egypt. Their first task was to prevent the ceiling of the vestibule from collapsing; cleverly, they decided to support it with four wooden posts which they disguised as columns covered with beautifully polished stucco, thus giving the room the appearance of a Roman atrium. In order to link the reception rooms together, they conceived the idea of opening up the arcades leading to the billiard room and the dining room with a system of sliding mirrors.

Pages 22–23: In 1806 the Empress Josephine helped Berthault obtain the post of architect for the palace of Compiègne. The renovations (which included replanting the garden) took several years. Berthault designed remarkable interiors for the apartments of the Emperor, the Empress and the King of Rome. The former Grand Staircase of the Queen, which had been completed in 1784, led to the King of Rome's apartment: in 1808 Berthault added two gilt bronze torchères and, on the landing, an iron stove supporting a cast of the Apollo Belvedere.

Pages 24–25: The staircase in the Élysée Palace, then the residence of Joachim Murat, is all the more remarkable because few staircases were built in the Empire period. Designed by the architects Jean-Thomas Thibault (1757–1826) and Barthélémy Vignon (1762–1846), it consists of a first flight of twenty-three steps leading to a landing from which two more flights rise to a vestibule on the first floor. The palm-leaf balusters emerge from olive wreaths, all in bronzed and gilt lead; the sheet-metal handrail was made by the firm of Blaise-Louis Deharme, founded in 1791, which specialized in varnished, gilded and painted metal for use in furniture.

Furniture

The abolition of the guilds in 1791 did away with the distinction between cabinetmakers and joiners, and from then on, craftsmen were free to make furniture of their own choice – as did the Jacob brothers between 1796 and 1803, and Jacob-Desmalter who succeeded them. Most of the furnishings supplied to the imperial palaces were made in their workshops, and their furniture – often designed by Charles Percier – was much in demand. Other furniture-makers, such as Marcion, Brion and Lignereux, were also commissioned; the latter sold his business to Thomire, who soon linked up with Duterme, and, as well as doing a great deal of work in bronze, made console tables, jardinières and secretaires.

Furniture made between 1795 and 1805 was usually of mahogany, sometimes enhanced by the brightness of lemonwood, and ornamented with motifs in ebony, pewter, mother-of-pearl and brass. It was only with the appearance of the *Étiquette du Palais Impérial*, drawn up in 1805, that its design and decorative vocabulary underwent a change. Forms tended to become heavier and more solid. Elegant curves gave way to straight lines in chair backs; simple, tapering legs were replaced by heavier legs with double baluster turning; armrests began to scroll; and armchair backs curved into the so-called gondola shape. Decorative motifs became more and more insistent, gradually covering

Top: Heads with *nemes* headdresses in blackened wood, and other Egyptian-inspired motifs in ebony, decorate a commode attributed to the Jacob brothers, originally in Josephine's apartment in the Tuileries.

Above: Burr cedar, mahogany and ebony add character to this secretaire, completed in 1806 by Simon-Nicolas Mansion, along with a matching commode. Both were presented to Napoleon by the City of Paris on his birthday, 15 August 1806.

Left: A cheval glass delivered in 1811 for the apartment of the King of Rome, subsequently placed in Queen Marie-Amélie's bedroom in the Grand Trianon at Versailles in 1834. The use of ash for the frame reflects the Emperor's wish to favour native French woods over mahogany.

Opposite: A remarkable secretaire by Jacob-Desmalter: the brilliance of mahogany and the richness of yew root are heightened by the splendour of the gilt bronze decorations.

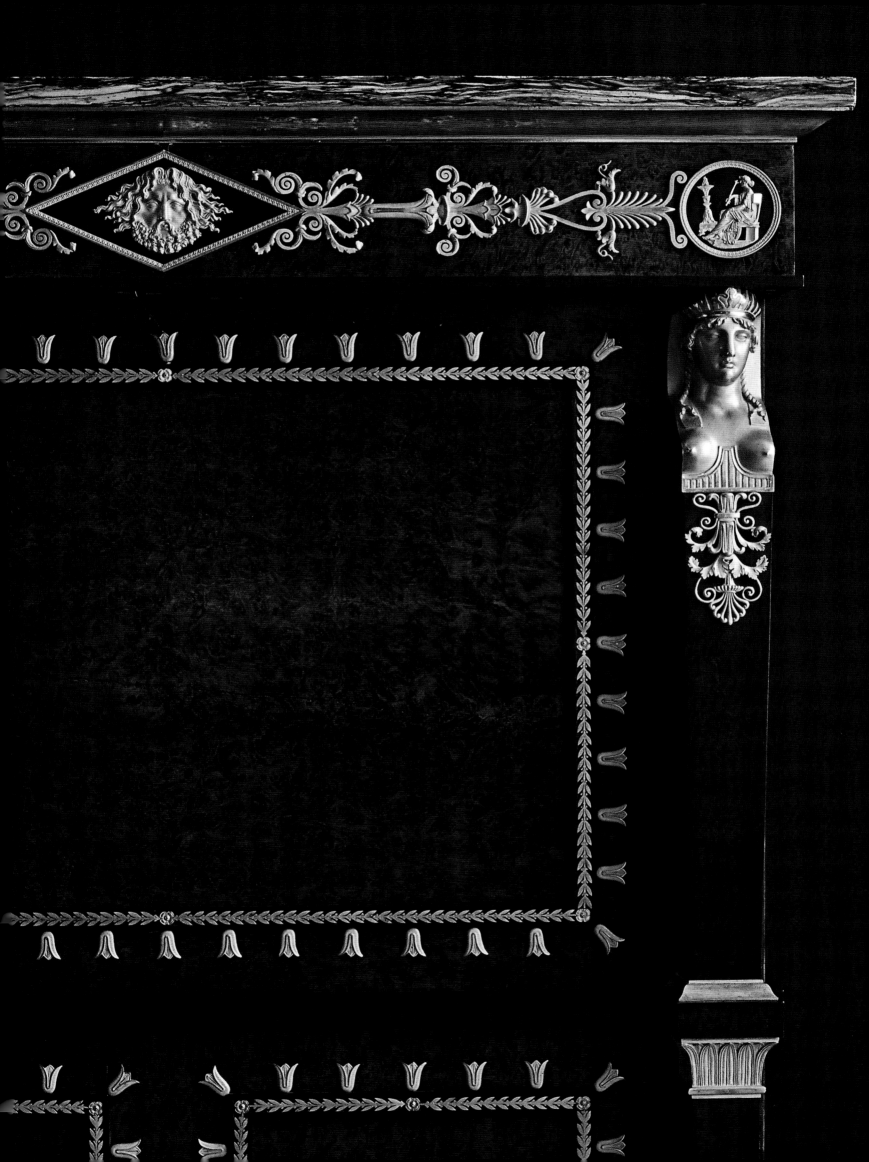

all the flat surfaces, as though the designers suffered from *horror vacui*. In reception rooms, mahogany was gradually supplanted by painted or gilded wood, not only because of the continental blockade, which made it difficult to get supplies, but also because the Emperor wished to promote the use of native woods: chairs, for instance, were generally made of beechwood. Cabinetmakers used burr cedar, elm or ash, and yew root, to make patterns with the grain. Napoleon ordered furniture in plane wood for his bathroom at Compiègne, and in amaranth for the Hameau of the Trianon at Versailles in 1811. The more easily available wood of fruit trees – wild cherry, pear and olive – met the needs of less well-to-do clients, and was used in many middle-class apartments.

Most of the furniture created by cabinetmakers was richly decorated with gilt bronze, and larger firms such as Jacob-Desmalter had their own bronze workshops. The motifs were usually applied on the surface in such as way as to enhance the grain of the mahogany. Paris was renowned for its bronze work at the time, the principal exponents being Thomire, Galle, Ravrio and Feuchère. There was no competition, and finished products were exported all over Europe, mainly to Russia, Spain, Italy and Great Britain. Apart from bronze decorations for furniture, the workshops produced a wide variety of clocks, candelabra, firedogs,

Opposite: Josephine's boudoir in the palace of Saint-Cloud was furnished with a sofa, four side chairs, and four armchairs with armrests in the form of swans, all upholstered in red velvet with rich gold embroidery. They were designed by Percier and made by Jacob.

Top: The swan motif that forms the arms of the chairs at Saint-Cloud was echoed in gilded wood and with slight variations on the chairs of the main bedroom in the Hôtel de Beauharnais in Paris.

Above: Twelve of these elegant chairs were made in the workshops of the Jacob brothers around 1803, and acquired by Murat in 1805 for the library of the Elysée Palace. Their curving backs, of mahogany and lemonwood inlaid with ebony and pewter, give them a character of great refinement.

Top: The seats in the music room at Malmaison, covered in red wool with a black velvet trim, have armrests fronted by winged female heads. The set, made around 1800, bears the struck mark of the Jacob brothers; it comprised four sofas, four armchairs and two X-frame stools.

Above: For the drawing room at Malmaison, around the same time, the Jacob brothers created a large set of furniture comprising two sofas, two bergères, eight armchairs and twelve side chairs, all covered in blue silk velvet with rich gold trimmings. Unusually, the armrests do not rest directly on the Egyptian-style heads, creating a more elegant effect than in later versions.

Top: The monumental nature of this stool links it to a commission, entrusted to Martin-Guillaume Biennais (1764–1843), for stools for the marshals, intended to stand near the Emperor's throne. The legs have the form of crossed sabres in mahogany, with ebony handles ending in lionesses' heads of richly chiselled gilt bronze.

Above: This type of X-frame stool was inspired by the curule chair, used by Roman magistrates. The Jacob brothers made a set of ten for the council chamber at Malmaison, and made more for several military men in Napoleon's entourage, including Moreau, Murat and Mortier.

Top: A bed made by Jacob-Desmalter in 1806 for Prince Eugène's bedroom in the Tuileries in Paris. The head and foot are identical, crowned with female heads of classical inspiration.

Above: This elegant bedside cabinet known as a *somno*, ornamented with a sleeping dog in gilt bronze, was made by Jacob-Desmalter in 1804. In 1808 the firm also supplied the seating for this bedroom in the Empress's private apartment at Fontainebleau: the weighty scrolled armrests in gilded wood announce the style of the Restoration.

Top: This remarkable tea table was commissioned in 1801 by the Minister of the Interior, Chaptal, to encourage Deharme's work in varnished metal. A combination of varnished sheet metal, steel, and gilt and patinated bronze, it juxtaposes Egyptian motifs with reliefs that are still in Louis XVI style.

Above : This fender, surmounted by a sphinx in gilt and patinated bronze, was made under the Consulate, and comes from the Minister of State's apartment in the palace of Saint-Cloud. It is attributed to the bronze-caster Claude Galle (1759–1815), a great rival of Thomire.

Left: A spectacular clock, depicting Jason and the Golden Fleece. It was described in the *Journal des dames et des modes* of 25 August 1819, which concluded: 'All in all, the work is in fine taste and it is a superb item of salon furniture.'

Opposite: The Emperor's salon in the Grand Trianon at Versailles was, in accordance with imperial palace etiquette, the most richly furnished room of all. It was known as the Salon des Malachites, because Napoleon chose to place here the furniture decorated with malachite that the Russian Tsar Alexander I had given him by after the Treaty of Tilsit. The other furniture, including the stools and chairs covered in damask with an oak-leaf motif, were made by Jacob-Desmalter in 1810, and have never left the room since the days of the Empire.

candlesticks, torches, sconces and torchères. Clocks were an important part of the repertoire. The simplest were in the shape of a vase or a milestone, or based on architectural forms, but there were others devoted to themes ranging from allegory to mythology, or based on sculptures such as Falconet's *Melancholy*, or on famous paintings such as David's *Oath of the Horatii*. The fob watch, however, remained the most common means of telling the time, and clocks remained a luxury. There were only 66 of them in the 1,500 rooms of the palace of Fontainebleau, and a mere 12 at Malmaison. A really fine clock could cost some 4,000 francs – more if its design was unique – and even the simplest could cost up to 1,000 francs. The wages of a gardener at the time were just 600 francs a year.

Firedogs or andirons were a decorative feature of fireplaces and were also made of bronze, except for the bars used to support the burning logs, which were in cast iron. They could take a variety of forms, ranging from simple egg, apple or ball shapes to elaborate animal figures, including sphinxes, lions and griffins. They sometimes featured gilt images in relief against a bronze ground.

This was also the time when sheet metal began to be used in furniture. The firm of Deharme, later succeeded by Tavernier, supplied Murat with a large tea table in 1801, and then made the handrail of the staircase for the Élysée Palace (see pages 24–25), as well as vases of different sizes, clock cases and torchères. Sheet metal could be painted to resemble malachite, porphyry or granite.

Left: Percier designed a jewelry cabinet for the Empress Josephine in 1806, but it was not delivered until three years later, just before her divorce. A detail of the finished cabinet, known as the 'Grand Ecrin', is shown overleaf (for the caption, see page 46).

PREVIOUS PAGES

Pages 36–37: Josephine's jewelry cabinet, known as the 'Grand Écrin', was one of the most expensive items of furniture ever made by Jacob-Desmalter. Commissioned in 1806 for the Empress's state bedroom in the Tuileries, it was not finished until 1809, shortly before the divorce. Its secret mechanisms were changed, and it passed to Marie-Louise. Made of exotic woods including mahogany, yew, amaranth and ebony, it is decorated with mother-of-pearl and splendid gilt bronze from the Jacob workshops. The piece was designed by the ubiquitous Percier, but the bronzes are due to the sculptor Denis-Antoine Chaudet (1763–1810). The central subject was inspired by a relief by a follower of Jean Goujon, representing 'The birth of the Queen of the Earth, to whom putti and goddesses hasten to bring offerings'; other bronze motifs allude to dress and jewelry.

Pages 38–39: The desk in the form of a triumphal arch, commissioned in 1797 by Josephine for her house in the rue de la Victoire and was made by the Jacob brothers to a design by Percier, is unique. It was accompanied by a commode decorated with the same

bronze scrolls and griffins, possibly based on drawings of ancient monuments that Percier and Fontaine had made in Rome. The four winged victories in patinated bronze give the piece an unrivalled monumentality. After she had become Empress, Josephine had the two pieces placed in her boudoir in the Tuileries. In 1810, however, they were separated: the bureau was moved to the boudoir in the Grand Trianon, and the commode to Fontainebleau, its bronze ornaments being transferred to another item.

Pages 40–41: The state bedroom on the first floor of Prince Eugène de Beauharnais's *hôtel* was furnished with ostentatious luxury. The table is remarkable, with thyrsus motifs painted in gouache. On it stands a bust of Queen Hortense, by François-Joseph Bosio – a reminder of the fact that this room was said to have been hers originally, although there is no evidence for that claim. The walls, six armchairs with swans, a bergère, and six side chairs of gilded carved wood were originally covered in green velvet with gold embroidery; that was replaced by silk, of which we now see a copy rewoven in the 1960s.

Pages 42–43: The Grand Salon on the first floor of the Hôtel de Beauharnais is the most richly furnished room in the house. The table of sheet metal painted to simulate green granite, supported by two chimeras in gilded wood, stands facing the fireplace. Of the twenty-three armchairs, twenty-four side chairs and a sofa of gilded wood, all attributed to Pierre-Antoine Bellangé (1758–1827), however, not all remain. Modern silk replaces their original covering in blue *gros de Naples* with silk embroidery.

Pages 44–45: Still standing on the mantelpiece of the music room in the Hôtel de Beauharnais is this clock by Joseph Revel, who received his master's certificate in 1775 and was still active in 1810. The figure in patinated bronze represents the Greek poetess Sappho, carrying her lyre and leaning on a pedestal of gilt bronze.

THESE PAGES

Above: The large octagonal table with a green marble top, now in the Emperor's salon at Malmaison, was acquired on the order of Napoleon III at a public sale in the Hôtel Drouot in 1866. He had decided to refurnish the château, which he had bought completely empty five years earlier, and the table was then believed to have come from a sale at Malmaison in 1818. It may however be the 'octagonal table in marble of various colours, with in the centre a bird inlaid in white marble', which was recorded as being in the music room in 1824, at the death of Prince Eugène, with its marble top replaced at an unknown date.

Opposite: A luxury edition of Percier and Fontaine's *Recueil comprenant tout ce qui a rapport à l'ameublement de décorations intérieures* (Compendium of all things connected with the furnishing of interiors), decorated in watercolour in 1825 by Benjamin Gotthold Schlick (1796–1872), and bound by Joseph Thouvenin (d. 1854).

RECUEIL

Comprenant tout ce qui a rapport

A L'AMEUBLEMENT

de Décorations Intérieures

comme

VASES, TRÉPIEDS, CANDELABRES, CASSOLETTES,

POÊLES, PENDULES, TABLES, SECRÉTAIRES,

LUSTRES, GIRANDOLES, LAMPES, CHANDELIERS, CHEMINÉES, FEUX,

LITS, CANAPÉS, FAUTEUILS, CHAISES, TABOURETS,

MIROIRS, ÉCRANS, &c.

Dining rooms

A relative newcomer to the domestic scene, the dining room emerged at the beginning of the 17th century from the combination of the medieval great hall and the anteroom; it started to become a regular feature in the residences of the aristocracy during the First Empire. The earliest records of separate rooms for eating seem to date from the reign of Louis XIII (1610–43), but they were unusual then even in royal residences; people had their meals on folding tables set up in the anteroom or even in the bedroom, depending on the number and status of those present. Generally, where one ate was determined by the size of the dwelling: in the simplest houses people still ate in the kitchen, which was the warmest room. A taste for comfort developed in the early 18th century, and the dining room became a common feature in the upper echelons of society, though Versailles did not get its first one until 1735, in the *petits appartements* of Louis XV. By the second half of the century, however, they became a necessity in every great house.

The dining rooms of the imperial palaces all had rich wall decoration. Stucco was much in favour because it did not retain odours, whereas cloth did. In wealthy private households, most rooms were wood-panelled, and walls were punctuated with shelves of white marble. In more modest homes, the walls might be covered with wallpaper imitating white marble, and the shelves would be of wood covered with waxed cloth. The floor was usually paved, either with octagonal flagstones or with a chequerboard pattern of marble. This was washed once a week with soft soap to give it a bright, polished appearance. In keeping with the old adage that 'one does not age at table', there were no clocks in these dining rooms, and as it was felt that an open fire was not a suitable sight for guests, fireplaces were usually replaced by square or cylindrical ceramic stoves, with marble tops on which plates could be warmed. In order to maintain a comfortable temperature until about three o'clock in the afternoon, the stoves were fired up at eight o'clock in the morning; and they needed to be stoked again for the evening. Larger houses had *calorifères* (iron heating pipes) in the cellars, which provided a gentle form of heating for the rooms above. This system, similar to Roman hypocausts, was revived at the beginning of the 19th century, and architects such as Fontaine, Berthault and Thibault installed them in the houses they designed. The composer Félix Blangini, while waiting one day in the dining room at Malmaison to see the Empress Josephine, noted that the floor 'was paved with large flagstones beneath which lay a *calorifère*. No doubt the person in charge of heating had doubled, or rather tripled, the amount of coal in order to spread a healthy heat throughout

Opposite: The dining room of the Hôtel Bourrienne is the only room in the house that looks out on both the courtyard and the garden. It is divided into two by four columns, so that part of it can also be used as a salon. The beautiful parquet flooring of rosewood, lemonwood and mahogany is answered on the walls by four sculpted panels with nymphs.

the rooms, but it certainly wasn't healthy for my feet. I was wearing very thin shoes, and the heat from the flagstones was so intense that I was constantly forced to change position, so that I looked like a dancer in the famous ballet of the Turkeys . . . I don't know what would have become of me in that scalding situation if the Empress hadn't sent for me soon.'

These basic rules were also applied in the imperial residences, except at Fontainebleau, where the walls were covered with Gobelins tapestries and there was a large clock with nine dials. After all, in the words of Napoleon, this was the 'house of centuries'. At Compiègne, Berthault covered the Empress's dining room walls with fine stucco simulating antique yellow marble, and all round the room was a band of bluish-grey marble that concealed a heating pipe. Percier and Fontaine did the same at Malmaison, commissioning Lafitte to paint a series of Pompeian dancers on the stucco walls, and at Saint-Cloud, where the handsome dining room is decorated with stucco work by Zobel and decorative paintings by Moench (known as Munich). Where it was possible to pipe water, there would also be a fountain, whose function was both decorative and utilitarian.

Among the *nouveaux riches* and kept women, the luxury of dining rooms became frankly vulgar, such as that of Mlle Dervieux, the celebrated dancer at the Opéra, who in 1789

commissioned the architect Bélanger to create a sumptuous setting in antique style in which large mirrors alternated with mahogany balusters. When Louis Bonaparte and Hortense de Beauharnais moved into the house in 1802, the style was still so fashionable that they did not change a thing. More modestly, the little house in the rue de la Victoire that Josephine rented in 1795 contained just one small salon which also served as a dining room; it had a simple marble pedestal table and a round mahogany table, and the dishes were squeezed into two glass-fronted cabinets.

With the rise of the bourgeoisie came the spread of apartment buildings that sought to replicate the aristocratic *hôtel*. They tended to include dining rooms, but these were

Above: In middle-class houses, instead of porcelain there was often fine earthenware. This initially came from England; it was not until the years 1792–1804 that five factories making 'English-style' ceramics opened in the suburbs of Paris. They enjoyed an immediate success thanks to their low prices and their use of printed designs that made possible a wide variety of patterns.

not yet regarded as principal rooms, so they often over-looked the street. The bourgeois were keen to emulate the lifestyle of the nobility, but often ended up merely mimicking it, putting three, four or five chairs round the table of their would-be dining room, thus making it virtually impossible to move around. For servants to do their work efficiently, the distance between table and walls needed to be about 1 metre (3 ft) at the ends of the room and about 1.3 metres (4 ft) at the sides; the recommended total area was 13–19 m² (140–205 sq. ft) for a small apartment, 28–38 m² (300–410 sq. ft) for a medium-sized one, and 45–69 m² (485–743 sq. ft) for a large one.

Most households made do with a folding table in the anteroom. The wife of the sculptor Jean-Guillaume Moitte did this in her apartment on the quai Malaquais, despite its generous size, confiding to her diary: 'We made great arrangements to dine in the second anteroom.' Things had not changed by the middle of the century, when Balzac wrote in his novel *La Cousine Bette*, published in 1847: 'Hortense was accommodated in the dining room, arranged as a bedroom with the help of the Maréchale's money, and the anteroom became the dining room, as it is in many apartments.'

Wherever it was located, the dining room had to be furnished with austere simplicity. In the apartments of people who were reasonably well-off, there was always a central table, either round or oval, surrounded by numerous chairs and console tables; there was also, if space allowed, a table for serving or carving and a plate-warmer, both usually masked by a screen. The serving table was placed in the corner nearest to the door leading to the kitchen, and if possible the console tables faced the sides of the table.

The room and furnishings had to be kept spotlessly clean and well ventilated in order not to retain the smell of food. The preferred mode of lighting was a chandelier, or a lamp with a reflector, suspended from the ceiling above the centre of the table, while candelabra of gilt bronze or silver-plated copper stood on the table itself.

It was the same in all the imperial residences, where there was always a large mahogany table with claw feet on casters, which could be extended indefinitely by means of inserted leaves. Although they might be inconvenient at table, etiquette demanded that there should be two arm-chairs, one for the Emperor and one for the Empress, and a varying number of chairs depending on the size of the residence: there were twelve only at Malmaison, twenty-four at Fontainebleau, forty at Saint-Cloud, and fifty at the Tuileries. These chairs were always made of mahogany and were sometimes covered with horsehair – a material that was hard-wearing but very slippery, and that damaged

51

delicate muslin and chiffon dresses; an alternative was morocco, which was easier to clean than silk upholstery in case of spills. Chairs made of walnut or cherry wood might have more modest cane or wicker seats. It was also customary for the ladies to rest their feet on little cushions made of straw or fabric, which were taken away as soon as the meal was over.

A similar layout was to be found in the homes of high-ranking military officers, as in the dining room of General Moreau's *hôtel*; there the furniture comprised a large table with sixteen legs ending in claw feet (capable of seating thirty), twenty-four chairs and three console tables.

Above: Percier and Fontaine's *Recueil de décorations intérieures*, published in 1801, had a great influence on the decorative arts throughout Europe at the beginning of the 19th century. This plate shows the decoration of the vault and of an arch in the dining room in the Tuileries Palace.

Opposite: The curved end of the dining room at Malmaison is articulated by eight pilasters, each decorated with a thyrsus and a floral crown from which a sconce projects. The little white marble fountain between the two dancers was surmounted by a statue of the goddess Hebe, which does not survive.

Left: Silversmiths such as Auguste, Odiot and Biennais borrowed techniques from bronze-casting and developed new, quicker methods which allowed them to compete more successfully with porcelain. To make serving easier, the pieces were often placed on console tables with shelves above, which were rather like dressers. Later, these were also given doors and stepped shelves, to produce the 'credenza'-like buffet that became an integral feature of every dining room from the second half of the 19th century onwards.

Opposite: In inventories drawn up during the Empire, the dining room in the Empress's apartment at Compiègne is also called the *premier salon*, denoting the sequence of the reception rooms. Its stucco walls and elegant plaster ceiling give it a simplicity appropriate to a dining room. The mahogany chairs by Jacob-Desmalter, covered in red morocco, stand out against the imitation leopardskin carpet, which is a recent reproduction. It was here, on the evening of 27 March 1810, that Napoleon burned his bridges, defied protocol, and took his first meal with Marie-Louise, accompanied only by his sister, Caroline, Queen of Naples, who had taken the place of the Empress's own grandmother, Queen Marie-Caroline.

PREVIOUS PAGES

Pages 54–55: This room in Malmaison was used as a dining room from the early 18th century on, when it was usual to set up a table temporarily in the anteroom for meals. It originally had only four windows. In 1800 Percier and Fontaine gave it a semicircular extension, and increased the number of windows to six. The main elements of the decoration are paintings on stucco of two antique tripods and eight dancers, executed by Louis Lafitte (1770–1828) to designs by Percier. The handsome black-and-white marble floor flows on into the vestibule and the billiard room, unifying the central rooms.

The furniture that was here during the Empire is now scattered, but its effect is suggested by an oval table and twelve chairs from the Tuileries and three console tables from Fontainebleau. The room is lit by two chandeliers of crystal and gilt bronze, each holding twelve candles, re-created in 1988.

Pages 56–57: For grand occasions, it was customary to create extravagant table decorations in glazed and coloured sugar, nougat and mastic, which might even take the shape of buildings; this pyramid of cakes is a more modest offering. The trend was started by the famous Antonin Carême,

master chef in Talleyrand's house during the Empire. He was involved in all the major events of the period, organizing the feasts that marked Napoleon's marriage and the birth of the King of Rome, and even directing the Tsar's kitchens during the occupation of Paris. In 1815 he published his first book, *Le Pâtissier royal parisien*, with a reference to Vignola's *Five Orders of Architecture*, clearly demonstrating the artistic ambition underlying his culinary skills.

Pages 58–59: The Empress's breakfast room in the palace of Compiègne is the only example of its kind to have survived intact, with the exception of the

Emperor's in the Grand Trianon. It was here that the Empress took her first meal of the day. Regarded as a private sanctuary, entered only by the sovereigns and their close companions, it is far less luxurious than the state apartments. The semicircular shape adds to its charm. The walls are covered with yellow lampas, which is also used for curtains that screened the doors to keep out draughts, and on the furniture – by Jacob-Desmalter – which is of painted rather than gilded wood. The room, furnished in 1809, was restored in 1981, the silk being rewoven by Tassinari et Chatel.

Tableware

The Empire was a fruitful period for the arts of the table. Be it porcelain, silver or crystal, everything was made in Paris, and the whole of Europe – with the exception perhaps of Britain – came to the French capital for its supplies.

After the Revolution, nothing was left of the royal silver, sent away to be melted down, or of the dinner services, all sold. As with the palaces, which had to be completely refurbished, tableware also had to start again from scratch. After Napoleon's coronation, the service used at court for official banquets was called the 'Grand Vermeil'. This was a vast set comprising over a thousand pieces, kept in sixty-three cases (only twenty-six pieces have survived; they are now at Fontainebleau). It was presented to the Emperor by the City of Paris on the occasion of his coronation, and was made by the silversmith Auguste. It was complemented by three other services, called 'Thé en vermeil', 'Vermeil de dessert' and 'Vermeil ordinaire', and a large silver-plated set – made mainly by Biennais – that was constantly supplemented throughout Napoleon's reign, providing tableware for up to three hundred people.

The factory at Sèvres produced two porcelain services for each of the royal residences: one for the entrée, consisting mainly of soup plates, butter dishes, salad bowls, jugs

Above: One of the largest porcelain factories in Paris was that of Darte Frères. In 1810 it employed sixty-eight workers, and this remarkable swan-shaped cup dates from that period. This design was very popular, and was also produced by Dagoty in Paris and by the Vista Alegre factory in Portugal.

Above: The Dagoty factory specialized in gold relief designs featuring Chinese figures and landscapes against a ground of red lacquer, as in this teacup and saucer. From 1804 onwards, the company enjoyed the patronage of the Empress Josephine.

Opposite: In *Portrait of a Woman drinking Coffee*, the artist Constance-Marie Charpentier (1767–1849) shows the woman holding a straight-sided Litron cup, designed specifically for coffee. It and the lidded sugar bowl on the table, with a yellow background and medallions imitating antique cameos, may well have come from one of the Parisian factories that were then exporting their products all over Europe.

Paris, which were often in competition with Sèvres – the most famous being Dihl et Guérhard, Dagoty, Nast, and Darte. Apart from tableware, these factories also produced 'cabarets', services used for breakfast in the morning or for afternoon tea. These usually consisted of a tea or coffee pot, cups of various shapes according to the beverage being drunk (coffee, tea or chocolate), a sugar bowl, a cream jug, a milk jug, and a larger bowl that could be used for milk with coffee and for punch at afternoon tea.

Those less well-off used earthenware, the production of which grew rapidly, thanks particularly to the spread of printed decoration, which had started in England and considerably lowered the price. Factories such as Creil, Choisy and Montereau offered their clients services with images on particular themes, including the monuments of Paris, ancient history, and the fables of La Fontaine.

The art of the silversmith underwent a similar development, as techniques were simplified, the different sections of a piece now being joined together by carefully concealed screws and rivets instead of the traditional soldering. Prices went down, and the rich middle classes and aristocrats were able to purchase impressive services made of silver or silver-gilt. Among the fifty or so silversmiths working in Paris around the rue Saint-Honoré, three names stand out: Auguste, Odiot and Biennais, who produced magnificent

and melon dishes, and the other – more richly decorated – for desserts, consisting of plates, fruit bowls, basins, sugar bowls and ice buckets.

The most famous of these dessert services was the one presented to the Emperor on the occasion of his marriage to Marie-Louise in 1810. Napoleon took it with him when he was exiled to St Helena. Other less sumptuous services were made for the palaces of Fontainebleau and Compiègne, and even for Stupinigi in Italy and Laeken in Belgium.

The products of the imperial factories were mostly reserved for the state, and wealthy individuals got their supplies from one of the nineteen porcelain factories in

Above: A cup and saucer from a coffee service made in 1810 on the occasion of Napoleon's marriage to Marie-Louise. It consisted of twenty-four cups and saucers, three sugar bowls, a creamer and a milk jug, all decorated with blue and gold hieroglyphs. The cups were painted with views of Egypt, and the saucers with heads of sheikhs. Napoleon took this service with him into exile on St Helena.

Opposite: Two Egyptian services were made by Sèvres during the Empire: the first was presented by Napoleon to Tsar Alexander I in 1808, and the second, made for the Empress Josephine, was given by Louis XVIII to the Duke of Wellington in 1818. All the plates reproduce illustrations from Vivant Denon's *Voyage dans la Basse et la Haute Egypte* (Travels in Lower and Upper Egypt): this is the 'Palace and Temples of Thebes at Medinet Habu'.

pieces not only for the Emperor and his entourage but also for numerous courts throughout Europe, including those of Russia, Bavaria, and various states in Italy.

Also essential for a table setting was glassware. It was not until 1781 that the French, at Saint-Louis, discovered the secret of crystal-making, and at last they were able to imitate the famous crystal of their English counterparts. It was, however, the old Montcenis factory at Le Creusot in Burgundy that cornered the market during the Empire. The director at the time was Ladouèpe du Fougerais, and his factory gained the patronage of the Empress Josephine, having previously enjoyed that of Marie Antoinette. As well as the traditional carafes for water and smaller carafes for spirits, they supplied the royal table with tumblers, champagne flutes, and a wide range of glasses for dessert wines, Malaga, liqueurs and even punch.

For ceremonial dinners, the table was decorated with a centrepiece, usually of chased, gilt bronze – Thomire was a specialist in this – or sometimes in biscuit porcelain, like that of the Egyptian service, 6.5 metres (21 ft) long, or that of the Emperor's private service, which comprised no fewer than twenty-five pieces. The number of elements in a centrepiece varied, but usually it included baskets, composed dishes, footed cups and candelabra, all standing on a large mirrored salver with a decorative border.

This was the period when *service à la russe* began to supplant the traditional style of *service à la française*. In the latter, all the dishes were brought to the table and served at the same time: soups and hors-d'oeuvres, starters and second courses, and cheeses, fruit, ice creams and desserts were scattered over the table. It was a major undertaking to get hold of the dish you wanted, and furthermore the food would very quickly get cold in spite of the lids that were meant to keep in the heat. It was the famous gastronome Grimod de La Reynière who, at one of the weekly meetings of his tasting panel (*jury dégustateur*), suggested that each course should be served to all the diners at the same time. This idea appealed to the Tsar's ambassador to Paris, Prince Kurakin, and in 1810 he adopted this new mode of serving meals, which became known as *service à la russe*. The two methods were used concurrently for a while, until finally the sequential 'Russian style' won the day.

Top: Before the invention of the first vapor-compression refrigerator, patented in 1857, ice was gathered from frozen lakes in winter and stored in icehouses, which were built in the shadiest part of a house's grounds or garden. Only people of the highest social rank had cups such as these, which were specifically designed for sorbets. Those illustrated bear the crowned 'J' of the Empress Josephine.

Above: With a taste as refined as that of her mother Josephine, Queen Hortense was the owner of cut-glass services that included these little carafes and liqueur glasses. The diamond cutting caught the light and helped to accentuate her monogram, the crowned 'H'. Hortense, Queen of Holland from 1806 to 1810, was the mother of Napoleon III.

Top and above: Between 1811 and 1813, the Empress Josephine commissioned a very ornate dessert service from the porcelain factory of Dihl et Guérhard. Her son, Prince Eugène, owned a similar but smaller one, and the two services were brought together when the Empress died. The plates were decorated with scenes based on Flemish and Dutch paintings in the gallery at Malmaison, European landscapes, and a large series of views of Italy. The collection was dispersed at the beginning of the 20th century, and half of it is now divided between the Hermitage in St Petersburg and the museum at Malmaison.

Top: In 1819 the goldsmith Jean-Baptiste-Claude Odiot (1763–1850) gave the government a number of bronzes, selected from what he considered to be the best of his designs. Prominent among them was this *pot à oille*, decorated with a swan with outspread wings – a subject he re-used for the spout of some of his teapots. The *pot à oille* was a large dish used for serving a type of meat and vegetable stew.

Above: This mustard pot, one of two delivered in 1811 by Biennais and bearing his mark, was part of what was called the 'petit vermeil', or ordinary silver-gilt ware, to distinguish it from the 'Grand Vermeil' presented in 1804 by the City of Paris. Both mustard pots are now in the museum at Fontainebleau.

Top: This sauceboat is one of two supplied by Biennais to Bonaparte as First Consul; the imperial coat of arms was added in 1806. With so many important commissions, Biennais subcontracted the work, and it bears the mark of the silversmith Marie-Joseph-Gabriel Genu. The Emperor took it with him to St Helena, and it was found there after his death in 1821.

Above: This cup, the work of Biennais, was part of a silver-gilt *nécessaire* or grooming set belonging to Napoleon, which he gave as a gift to Tsar Alexander I in 1808 at the Erfurt Conference. A single cup for personal use, it has the faceted shape with engraved flowers that is found in other *nécessaires* used by the Emperor.

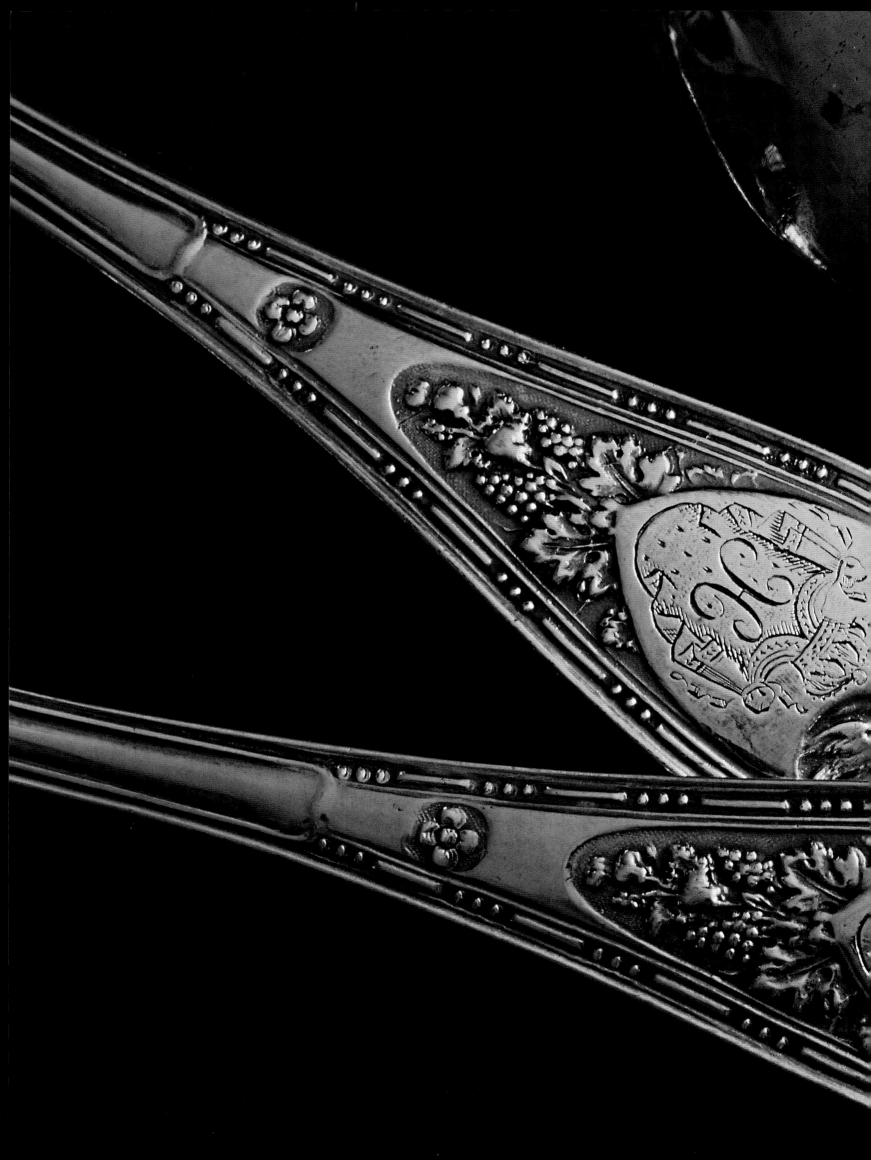

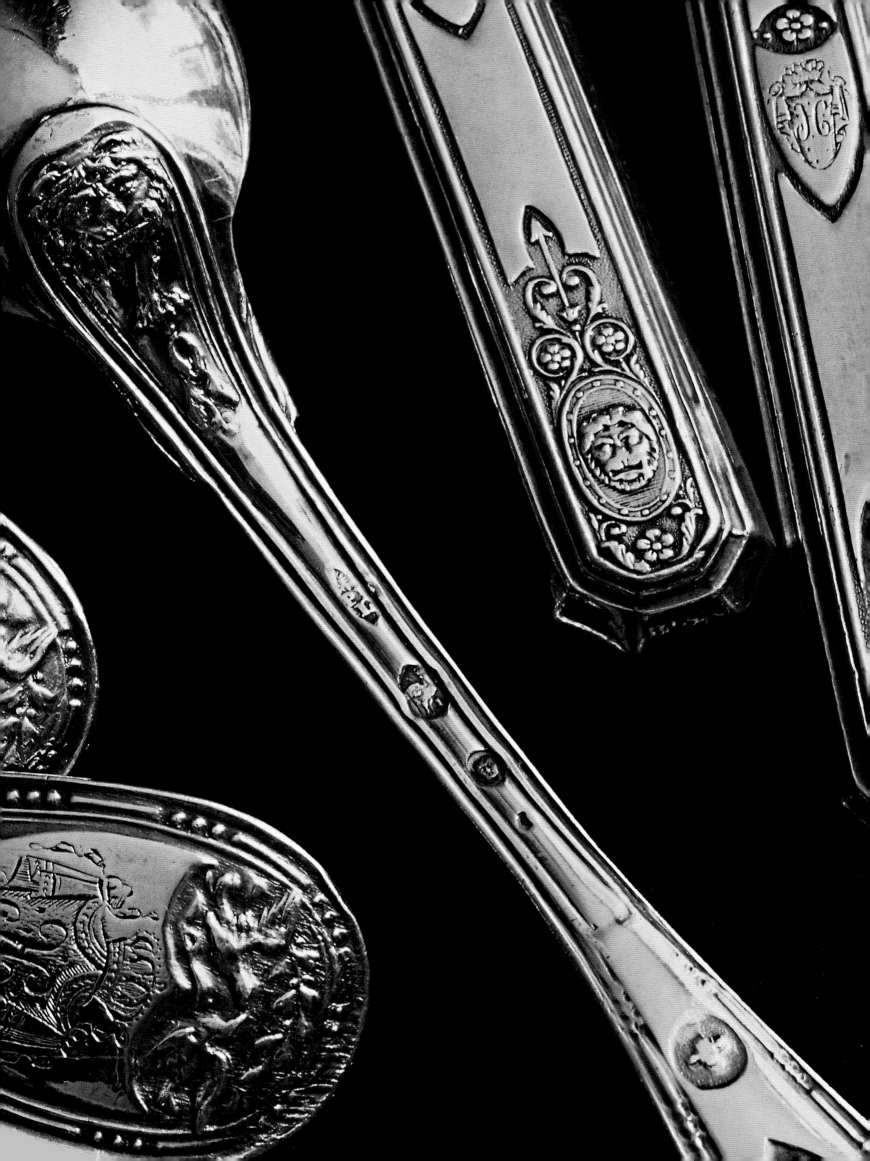

PREVIOUS PAGES

Pages 70–71: The cruet on the left, by Odiot, shows his great talent for incorporating classical female figures: two women, back to back with a column between them, each hold a bowl to contain salt or pepper. The design became very popular and was repeated many times, occasionally with slight variations, mainly for the Russian market.

The bowl on the right is what the Sèvres factory archives call an Egyptian milk bowl or simply an Egyptian bowl; first produced in 1808, it is a reproduction of an ancient Egyptian piece illustrated in Denon's *Voyage dans la Basse et la Haute Egypte*: the only modification was to add a base, for stability. This modern reproduction is an exact copy of the bowl in the Egyptian service supplied to the Empress Josephine on 29 December 1808, which has survived in its entirety and is now in the museum at Malmaison.

Pages 72–73: Every year, at the end of December, the Sèvres factory sent its most recent products to the Tuileries Palace, so that they could be presented as gifts to the imperial family, to allied sovereigns, or to ladies of the imperial entourage. This breakfast set for two people depicts the marriage of Napoleon and Marie-Louise as a cameo in an ornate, richly coloured setting. Painted in 1812 by Antoine Béranger, it was taken at once to the Tuileries, and was given as a Christmas present in 1813 to Augusta Amelia of Bavaria, the wife of Prince Eugène, Viceroy of Italy.

Pages 74–75: The products of the Dagoty factory were considered to be the most elegant and most sophisticated of their time; they were renowned for the beauty of their colours, as in this *cabaret* – a service for tea or coffee – where a matt black ground sets off the subtle colours of the birds pecking at fruit. The decoration was inspired by the wall paintings of Pompeii, and the forms are classical too, such as the sugar bowl supported on a tripod with lion-paw feet. The *cabaret*, meant for just one person, consists of a tray, a coffee pot, a sugar bowl, a milk bowl, and a cup with flared rim.

Pages 76–77: This cutlery formed part of the private travel canteen of Queen Hortense, wife of Louis Bonaparte, King of Holland; it bears the mark of the silversmith Pierre-Benoît

Lorillon, who helped Biennais to fulfil his many commissions. The set, of silver gilt, was meant for the personal use of the Queen: it comprises a sixteen-sided tumbler, a fork, two spoons, and three knives, all contained in a case covered in green velvet.

Pages 78–79: Three pieces – teapot, tea caddy and creamer –from a large tea service supplied by Biennais in 1810 for the marriage of Napoleon and Marie-Louise, which is now divided between the Louvre in Paris and the Royal Scottish Museum in Edinburgh. The general design of the set was provided by Percier, but Biennais engaged the former engraver to the Mint, Augustin Dupré, to provide the design of the relief on the tea caddy: it is based on an antique wall painting from the Villa of Maecenas in Rome, known as the 'Aldobrandini Wedding' (it belonged to Cardinal Aldobrandini), and was clearly intended to allude to the Emperor's recent marriage.

THESE PAGES

Above: This coffee set, called the 'Nankin yellow and purple service', was finished in 1803 and delivered in 1805 to Napoleon and Josephine. All the pieces bear the name 'Pestum': they were based on antiquities that Denon had sold to Louis XVI in 1785 to serve as models for the craftsmen of Sèvres. The straight-sided cups, known as Litron cups, were specifically intended for coffee.

Opposite: This superb breakfast set, designed in 1813 by the Sèvres sculptor Ferdinand Régnier, includes various classical motifs. The contrast between the white biscuit and the gold background looks forward to the style of the following period. Napoleon gave it as a Christmas present in 1814 to the Duchesse de Castiglione-Colonna, wife of Marshal Augereau.

Salons

The salon was the heir to the medieval great hall, which in 18th-century France had become the *salle de compagnie* or *salon d'assemblée*. It was only to be found in the wealthiest households, and the term *salon* itself did not come into use until the 1720s.

In bourgeois interiors of the early 19th century, the salon and the bedroom were the most important rooms in an apartment. Ideally, the salon would be square, with a door in the wall opposite the windows, and the fireplace in the middle of one of the two side walls. The heavier furniture would be made of mahogany covered with Utrecht velvet, and generally consisted of a sofa, two bergères, six armchairs and four side chairs; a piano would be opposite the fireplace. Among the more well-to-do, the furniture was often made of gilded wood, upholstered with tapestry or silk. The windows were decorated with pretty curtains of embroidered muslin with white fringe; in front of them there were usually curtains made of percale or silk, sometimes draped asymmetrically and held back by gilt hooks. The space between the windows would be filled by a console table surmounted by a mirror, facing the door. Another mirror, over the fireplace, was essential to reflect the light; below it on the mantelpiece there would be a clock flanked by porcelain vases or candelabra. When there were guests, card tables and a round pedestal table with a *flambeau*

couvert (a shaded candelabra) would be brought in, the latter table being for those who did not wish to play. If the salon was not panelled in wood, the walls would be decorated with wallpaper, which was less expensive than silk. The floor had to be covered with a carpet, which more often than not was made up of narrow strips sewn together, so as to fit the size of the room more easily.

The salon was the centre of social life. It was there that people received guests and pursued the occupations of their choice: conversation, music, needlework, reading, playing cards – the same activities in private homes as at the court.

Napoleon regarded the Tuileries Palace as the imperial sanctuary, and no expense was spared to give it the splendour necessary for the sovereign's main residence. The salons naturally played an important role. They were divided between those of the Emperor's own apartment, looking out onto the courtyard and used for private audiences, and those used for public affairs, which overlooked the gardens and consisted of a series of interconnected rooms. First came the Salle des Maréchaux, in the central pavilion; this led to the Salon Bleu, which in turn led to the Salon de la Paix, the Throne Room, the Emperor's Salon or Council Chamber, and the Galerie de Diane. Gatherings generally took place once a week at the Tuileries: some four to six hundred guests would arrive at around nine o'clock

Left: The room that provides the setting for this *Family Portrait* by Joseph-Marcellin Combette (1770–1840) contains furniture in a variety of styles. The chair, stool and pedestal table were up-to-date, whereas the secretaire and the little flat desk are of the Louis XVI period, and the clock with the figure of Time is of a type created at the beginning of the 18th century.

Opposite: The *salon de compagnie* or drawing room in the Hôtel Bourrienne, situated at the centre of the house, opens out to the garden through two windows and a door leading to a small flight of steps. The decoration is very refined, with a canopy-like ceiling, and candelabra painted on the doors. In order to give more light to the room, the doors leading to the vestibule are faced with mirrors.

in the evening and wait for Napoleon in the first salons, where the card tables had been set up. Around ten o'clock, the Emperor and Empress would make their way to the Salle des Maréchaux, where for about an hour and a half the dancers from the *corps de ballet* of the Opéra or members of the orchestra would put on a show – which was not always to the visitors' liking. Next they would all go to the Galerie de Diane for a quick supper, which took barely a quarter of an hour, and then they would return to the various salons, finally leaving at about half past twelve or one o'clock in the morning.

Music played an important part in social life, and there was no salon or family gathering without a recital of love songs or instrumental music. The lyrics and melodies of these songs were often very simple, which made them easy to learn, and they were an essential part of a well-bred lady's artistic repertoire. Queen Hortense earned herself quite a reputation in this sphere, as she wrote in her memoirs: 'My sole occupation in the retreat where I lived was composing sad love songs. I did this with ease. Even the bustle of a salon was not distracting to me. *Partant pour la Syrie* was composed at Malmaison while my mother was playing *trictrac*. It was quite successful and was sung during the war of 1809, as *La Sentinelle* was during the Spanish war. After that, with each campaign I was asked to write another, which I always did with some difficulty, because I didn't like to pass myself off as a writer – too shining a reputation for a feeble talent like mine.' The guitar or harp provided an accompaniment for singing, while the fortepiano was the favourite instrument for concerts; those made by the Érard brothers were used in the imperial residences, and some have survived. Once a week the Empress Josephine held concerts at Malmaison, though these were less formal than those at the Tuileries. She invited the finest musicians of the day – the harpist Naderman, the horn-player Duvernoy, and the flautist Tulou, as well as leading tenors such as Garat and Elleviou – to perform in her little theatre. Most palaces had theatres: there was a magnificent one in the Tuileries, built by Fontaine in 1807 and capable of holding up to 1,200 spectators; an ingenious piece of engineering enabled the floors of stage and auditorium to be brought to the same level, creating a ballroom 35 metres (115 ft) long and 15 metres (50 ft) wide.

Games were an integral part of the pleasures of salon life. Tables for various card games were therefore to be found in all the imperial palaces. At Compiègne, for instance, the Empress's second salon was set aside specifically for this purpose, and contained tables for *trictrac* (an early form of backgammon), *quadrille*, *bouillotte* and *piquet*;

Right: François-Louis Dejuinne (1786–1844) painted this picture of Juliette Récamier's salon in her small apartment in the Abbaye-aux-Bois, rue de Sèvres, where she held a literary *salon* attended by the greatest writers of the time, including Chateaubriand. Some of the furniture had been made by the Jacob brothers under the Directoire for her house in the rue du Mont-Blanc, and she had it moved here.

the table-tops were often removable, so that the tables could be transformed into writing desks. Napoleon was not too keen on card games and stuck to whist, though he never played for money, despite having introduced the practice to the court. Players were allowed to remain seated in the presence of the sovereign. Mme de Rémusat wrote: 'One sat down at the table for the sake of appearances, but more often than not one held the cards without looking at them, and simply chatted. The Empress Josephine liked playing, even when it was not for money, and she was very good at whist.' During the Empire, there was no château that did not have a billiard room. The game was confined almost exclusively to the people at court and the upper middle classes, and the imperial palaces naturally kept up with the vogue. There was a billiard table in the salon of the Empress's private apartment at Fontainebleau, and another at Malmaison. Napoleon is known to have disliked the game, and on St Helena he used the billiard table to spread out his maps. Josephine, on the other hand, used to play a game before breakfast. Between 3 and 4 metres (10–13 ft) long, billiard tables were substantial pieces of furniture, with their six pockets (called *blouses*) to receive the ivory balls.

The word *salon* came to be used not just for the room but also for the gathering of high society people there. However, there were also many lords and financiers who staged concerts and balls every day in their gilded salons without necessarily 'holding a *salon*'. For this, in addition to social rank and wealth, one needed a wife to do the honours – a woman of character, education, and especially wit. The mistress of the house had to bring enemies together, and to get rid of nuisances, which required a good deal of skill and spirit. The *salons* held by Mme de Staël and Mme Récamier were so powerful that Napoleon himself was wary of them. So much so that during the Empire, the true *salons* – intellectual, cynical, anti-authoritarian – fell out of existence; assemblies of this kind were allowed only to celebrate victories, listen to music, or read poetry. Such were the *salons* of the actress Mlle Contat, the painter Gérard, Comtesse Merlin, and the Empress Josephine herself, whose elegant gatherings were held at Malmaison and Navarre.

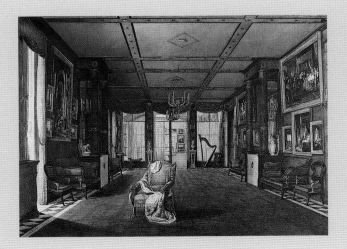

Left: With almost photographic precision, Auguste Garnerey captured every detail of the furniture, pictures and *objets d'art* which, by the end of the Empire, filled the music room at Malmaison. On view are the Empress's harp, the chairs made by the Jacob brothers, and the 'troubadour' style paintings of which Josephine was a passionate collector. At the back we glimpse the gallery, built in 1808, which does not survive.

THESE PAGES

Left: A portrait of the composer François-Adrien Boieldieu, by Louis-Léopold Boilly (1761–1845). Boieldieu (1775–1834) composed thirty-seven comic operas, including *Le Calife de Bagdad* (1800). He is shown standing in front of a Louis XVI-period fortepiano – an instrument that replaced the harpsichord in the 1760s, but did not develop in France until the first one was made by Sébastien Érard in 1778. The music of Mozart, Beethoven and Schubert was composed for the fortepiano, before the development of the pianoforte in the Romantic period.

Opposite: The music room at Malmaison contains two rare instruments from the château: Josephine's harp, made by Cousineau Père et Fils, and an unusual piano in the form of a secretaire, made by craftsmen from Germany, Pfeiffer and Petzold.

PREVIOUS PAGES

Pages 88–89: The Petit Salon, or Salon Bleu, in the Empress's apartment at Compiègne, was decorated in 1813–14 by the studio of Dubois and Redouté, so that Marie-Louise could have a room of her own that was more informal than the official reception rooms. The furniture of gilded wood, covered in blue moiré with gold embroidery, was made in 1812 by Jacob-Desmalter; the statue of *Innocence holding a Serpent to her Breast* is by Charles-Antoine Callamard.

Pages 90–91: When the Hôtel de Beauharnais was restored, the walls of the *anti-salon* on the first floor were covered with a crimson palm-leaf damask, rewoven by the firm of Tassinari et Chatel. (The *hôtel* had become the German embassy; at the beginning of the 20th century this room had been converted into a throne room, with a portrait of Kaiser Wilhelm II.)

Pages 92–93: The music room in the Hôtel de Beauharnais has appropriate decorative motifs on its doors, where medallions with portraits of the composers Gluck, Rameau, Haydn, Sacchini, Grétry and Paisiello are combined with various musical instruments. Bronze lyre motifs seen on the console table also decorated the backs of eight armchairs and sixteen side chairs of mahogany, lemonwood and amaranth, now replaced by chairs of gilded wood with swan-shaped armrests.

Pages 94–95: The *salon de compagnie* at Malmaison, also known as the Gold Salon, was decorated twice: first during the Consulate, and then in 1810–11. All that survives of the first scheme are the two large paintings of subjects from Ossian by Gérard and Girodet, and the fireplace, a gift from Pope Pius VII to Bonaparte as First Consul, now sadly stripped of its semiprecious stones and

mosaic. After her divorce, Josephine had the whole room redecorated by her architect, Berthault. He devised an elegant decor of white and gold, of which the doors and ceiling remain, and commissioned Étienne-Jean Delécluze (1781–1863) to paint six medallions on the subject of Daphnis and Chloe, four of which are back in position.

Pages 96–97: The Emperor's study in the Grand Trianon was created in 1812–13 in the space of two smaller rooms. It is situated in the private apartments, between the anteroom and the bathroom, and contains a fireplace of red marble from Italy, with rich bronzes by the famous metalworker Pierre-Auguste Forestier. Napoleon never saw it completed. The green and gold damask, decorated with fritillaries, was re-woven to the original design, which had been commissioned for the palace of Versailles in 1811 but never

used. The pedestal table comes from Murat's Élysée Palace, and the chairs from the First Consul's apartment in Saint-Cloud. The original chairs were sold off by the Domaines in 1875, but are gradually being bought back.

Pages 98–99: The third salon in the Empress's apartment at Compiègne was her main reception room, which explains the grandeur of the gilded wood furniture, comprising a sofa with two footstools, two bergères, ten armchairs, eighteen folding stools, six side chairs and a firescreen. Designed – as most of her furniture was – by Jacob-Desmalter, it was upholstered with green and gold brocade supplied at the beginning of 1809 by the firm of Grand Frères in Lyons, with a cornucopia motif in the form of the letter 'J'. The Empress Josephine never saw it installed, but despite the monogram, it remained after the arrival of Marie-Louise.

Textiles

Lyons silk, one of the great luxury industries, virtually died out during the Revolution. In January 1802 Napoleon as First Consul made an official visit to Lyons and, conscious of the need to revive the industry, commissioned Camille Pernon to supply a series of fabrics for Saint-Cloud. He took a personal interest, and later placed many more substantial orders, the largest being for the redecoration of Versailles, at a time when the Lyons silk industry was going through a serious crisis. Between 1810 and 1813, 80 kilometres (50 miles) of fabric left the Lyons workshops, creating a massive reserve on which governments that followed were able to draw, as late as the mid-

20th century. The Emperor also gave minor commissions to the factories in Tours, which were much smaller than those in Lyons. The types of textile were as varied as the range of colours: brocades, satins, *gros de Tours*, gourgourans, velvets, moirés, gold and silver *passementerie*, damasks and lampas were produced in crimson, blue, yellow, red, hazel, russet, lilac – and more. Official emblems such as the eagle, bee, imperial crown and cross of the Legion of Honour were very occasionally incorporated; but as with wallpaper, the most popular motifs were a great variety of flowers – fritillaries, asters, lilacs and roses – as well as more masculine symbols such as stars and

Above: This reproduction of the wall-hangings and curtains of the antesalon in the Hôtel de Beauharnais is a crimson version of the original green damask commissioned from Camille Pernon in Lyons for the First Consul's library at Saint-Cloud. They are framed by borders of gold brocade.

Above: The Salon Cerise on the first floor of the Hôtel de Beauharnais is situated between the Salon des Saisons and the bedroom. It owes its name to the cerise-coloured silk which covered the walls, curtains and chairs.

Opposite: The window curtains and those of the Emperor's bed in the bedroom at Compiègne were in gold brocade with a crimson base, decorated with palmettes and stars – a design that had been conceived for the bedroom at Saint-Cloud. It was rewoven by Tassinari et Chatel.

Top: This rich gold brocade on a blue ground with what was known as a 'Turkish' motif was commissioned in 1802 from Camille Pernon for Josephine's bedroom at Saint-Cloud. It was not delivered until 1806, and then the Empress rejected it because it was no longer to her taste. It was not used until 1809, for the bedroom of the prince's apartments at Compiègne, which later – in 1811 – became the bedroom of the King of Rome.

Above: The original design for this silver and blue satin brocade, decorated with rosettes, survives in the archives of the Maison Prelle in Lyons. 'Brocade' originally meant a textile entirely woven in gold and silver thread; later, it came to designate a silk textile interwoven with gold or silver thread.

Top right: Maison Prelle rewove this lampas with a pattern of lyres and swans, designed as a seat cover. It was originally commissioned in 1813 for the prefecture in Rome, in the palace of Montecitorio, then the residence of Napoleon's prefect Comte Camille de Tournon (the palace now houses the Italian Chamber of Deputies).

Bottom right: This yellow satin with crown imperial flowers was commissioned in 1808 from Bissardon, Cousin et Cie for the Emperor's bedroom in the palace of Meudon; it was rewoven to cover the chairs that had been made for that room in 1811 by the upholsterer Maigret, which are now in the museum at Fontainebleau.

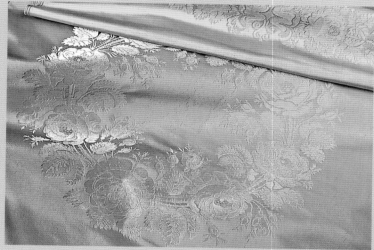

Top: This cut velvet on a blue satin ground, which probably dates from the beginning of the 19th century, is decorated with an antique vase and a helmet. This reproduction is by Prelle. The vase motif was repeated on another cut velvet, in green, commissioned in 1811 for the Empress's *cabinet de repos* at Versailles.

Above: This green *gros de Tours* with motifs of a rose and bees was commissioned in 1811 from Seriziat et Cie in Lyons for the *cabinet de repos* of the Emperor at Versailles; completed in 1813, it was used during the Restoration to cover a set of chairs for the palace of Fontainebleau. It too has been rewoven by Prelle.

Top: A textile designed in 1813 as a seat cover. The naturalistic treatment of the rose garlands on a yellow ground heralds the designs of the following period, which gradually departed from the symmetrical motifs characteristic of the Empire period. This too is a recreation by Prelle.

Above: This damask with a Greek key and hydrangea design, originally woven in yellow, lilac and white, was commissioned in 1811 from Chuard et Cie for the first salon of Marie-Louise's apartment at Versailles. It was delivered in 1813, but not used until the Restoration, at the Tuileries and Saint-Cloud. This recreation, again by Prelle, has a red ground.

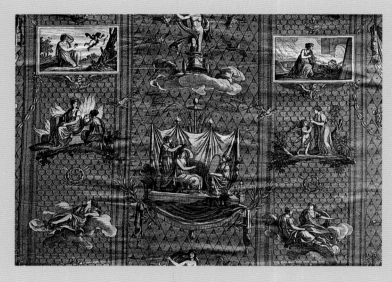

laurel, palm and oak leaves. These textiles were used to cover both walls and chairs, and the motifs were repeated in borders, which articulated the various parts of the furnishings. The same border motifs were used to edge curtains, which were often of plain silk slub, decorated with elaborate braids and trimmings.

Silk was reserved for the elite, and most people used printed cottons, which continued to be manufactured in several regions of France, the best-known being those produced by Oberkampf at Jouy. These rivalled English

textiles, and Napoleon took a great interest, going so far as to say to Oberkampf: 'You and I are waging a fine war against the English, you with your industry and me with my weapons – but you are the more successful.'

Napoleon also gave his support to other imperial factories, as witness a note written in 1807 by Duroc concerning the furnishing of the Tuileries: 'His Majesty wishes the following rule to be adhered to in this project: textiles from Lyons are to be used for the ground floor of the Empress's apartments, and the furnishings of the Great Apartment are to come from the Gobelins, Beauvais and the Savonnerie.' The Gobelins factory had the most important role, and their looms produced a series of tapestries celebrating Napoleon's reign, as they had already done for Louis XIV. The Beauvais factory, which specialized in upholstery, supplied coverings for benches, stools, armchairs and side chairs. Despite its size, the Savonnerie was able to supply only relatively few carpets, because they took so long to make; Napoleon therefore turned to two major private firms, those of Aubusson and Tournai, which in addition to knotted carpets made many composed of strips with geometric designs sewn together and surrounded by a border that was usually decorated with palmettes.

MANUFACTURE DE
PRES VERSAILL

N° 10
N° 14 a 160 V

24
100

PREVIOUS PAGES

Page 108: This damask with bee and oak-leaf motifs was commissioned from Camille Pernon in 1806 for the Palace of Versailles. It was eventually used at Compiègne for the Emperor's bedchamber as a wallcovering and to upholster the seating. The design was reissued by Tassinari et Chatel in 1976.

Page 109: In 1810 the joiner Pierre-Gaston Brion delivered a set of furniture in gilded wood for the Second Salon of the Emperor's private apartments at Fontainebleau. It consisted of a couch, a corner chair, a bergère, ten armchairs, twelve side chairs, a screen and a firescreen, all covered in rich green cut velvet with a pattern of palmettes, rosettes and flower vases.

Page 110: A satin border, commissioned in 1802 from Camille Pernon in Lyons for the First Consul's map room in Saint-Cloud, was used in 1809 for the small bedroom in the apartment known as the *double de Prince* at Compiègne, and it was rewoven for Compiègne by Tassinari et Chatel.

Page 111: This magnificent silver and blue brocade, with wreaths of myrtle and ivy, was part of the first commission given to Camille Pernon in 1802 for Josephine's Grand Salon at Saint-Cloud. It was later used for her Grand Salon at the Tuileries. In order to bring out the full beauty and richness of the hangings, the whole room had to be gilded. Josephine did not get to enjoy it for long, because it was installed only six months before her divorce.

Page 112: A copy rewoven by Tassinari et Chatel of a damask with a bee motif, originally on a white ground, commissioned in 1809 from Grand Frères in Lyons for the Emperor's study in the Tuileries. With the fall of the regime, the bee motif became unacceptable.

Page 113: This silk border of brocade and chenille with a running pattern of acanthus leaves and flowers was part of a textile made in Lyons at the end of the Ancien Régime by the firm of Gaudin and, after the latter had gone bankrupt, by Savournin. It was bought in 1790 by the royal furniture repository, but was not used until 1805, for the Empress's bedroom at Fontainebleau. The hangings and borders were rewoven between 1968 and 1986 by the firms of Prelle and Tassinari et Chatel in Lyons.

Pages 114–15: This damask with stars and imperial flowers was commissioned from Chuard et Cie in 1811 for three apartments in the palace of Versailles, in three colourways – crimson, yellow and white, and green, the latter being used in 1813 for the Emperor's private study in the Grand Trianon. This reproduction, also in green, was woven by Prelle and installed in 1965.

Page 116: The fabric chosen for the walls and seating in the Emperor's private salon at Fontainebleau, later known as the Salon de l'Abdication, is a rich crimson brocade with rose and lyre motifs. Made in 1809 by Cartier Fils, due to its dilapidated state it was replaced in 1999 by this version, rewoven by Prelle.

Page 117: Four armchairs, six side chairs, thirty folding stools, screen and firescreen in the Council Chamber at Fontainebleau were all upholstered in 1808 with a crimson damask decorated with crowns and stars commissioned in 1804 from Camille Pernon for Napoleon's bedroom at Saint-Cloud. The complete set was rewoven by Tassinari et Chatel between 1966 and 1972.

Pages 118–19: A carpet commissioned from Aubusson in May 1808, delivered the following February for the Empress Josephine's bedroom in the Tuileries. All that survives is the central section: the eagles and other symbols of the Emperor were removed at the Restoration. The factory at Aubusson was directed by Jean Sallandrouze de La Mornaix (1762–1826). Some of his carpets were designed by Jacques-Louis de La Hamayde de Saint-Ange-

Desmaisons, known as Saint-Ange (1780–1860). A pupil of Percier and of Brongniart, Saint-Ange worked chiefly for the Savonnerie, the Gobelins, and Sèvres.

THESE PAGES

Left: A tapestry portrait of the Empress Josephine, one of only two made at the Gobelins factory during the Empire, both of them based on paintings by François Gérard. Woven between 1808 and 1810, it shows her in her coronation regalia; it was completed after her divorce and given to Prince Eugène. The first, showing her wearing a day dress, was finished in 1809 and is modelled on the painting exhibited at the Salon in 1801; the Emperor gave it to Queen Hortense in 1811 (it is now in the museum at Malmaison).

Left, below: Architects such as Charles Percier (responsible for this design) painted cartoons in gouache for carpets that showed half or a quarter of the pattern, which was then repeated symmetrically.

Opposite: Popular decorative motifs of the Empire, such as the swan and the basket of flowers, went on being used: an inscription on the back of this carpet design notes that it was 'to be delivered 15 October 1838'.

Bedrooms

From the humblest to the richest of homes, the bedroom was the heart of every household. Primarily, of course, it was a place for sleeping, but it could also be a place to receive visitors, serving as a kind of private salon. This social function had its origin in the 17th century, when ladies would receive visitors in their bedrooms in the morning, the guests congregating in the space around the bed. The most celebrated of these ladies were the so-called Précieuses, who included the Marquise de Rambouillet and Ninon de Lenclos. This custom explains the many chairs that were always to be found in bedrooms. The bedchamber of the King of Rome at Compiègne contained no fewer than twelve armchairs, while that of the Emperor at Fontainebleau had eleven. Even the wife of General Moreau had ten chairs crowded into her bedroom. In both the imperial residences and the homes of the rich, the bedroom was the showpiece of luxury, with the bed – which in those days was called a *couchette* – as the crowning glory. It always stood on a platform, of mahogany or pine draped with cloth; textiles took pride of place, and the *tapissier* was the most highly prized of craftsmen.

Generally, couples would have separate bedrooms. Napoleon and Josephine, who shared a bed in somewhat bourgeois fashion, were an exception. The English visitor James Forbes made a point of this when in 1803 he noted that at Malmaison, 'in defiance of the French fashion of different apartments and separate beds, the First Consul and his lady repose under the same canopy.'

The separation of bedrooms gave architects a chance to use their imaginations in matters of furnishings and decoration. It was right and proper for Monsieur to have a room that was sober, even austere, usually with a somewhat military decor, and a bed, without a tester, standing on a simple platform.

Madame's room, on the other hand, would be more ornate. The bed usually had a canopy consisting of silk

Above: An Empire bedroom recreated for the Universal Exhibition in Paris of 1900, seen in an illustration after a gouache by Georges Rémon.

Opposite: In this painting by Marguerite Gérard, *The Nursing Mother*, the wooden bedframe has completely disappeared under the abundant bedding – the base, two wool mattresses, a feather mattress, a bolster, a pillow, sheets, coverlets, and counterpane, not to mention the curtains round the bed that keep out cold draughts.

curtains suspended from a crown. In the Empress Josephine's bedroom in the Tuileries Palace, where blue was the dominant colour, the bed was placed in an alcove with inner curtains that were blue with a very slight white tinge, and outer curtains that were white with a slight blue cast, edged with crests and fringe in blue and gold silk; the sloping top was draped with festoons, and the whole alcove was decorated with braid, fringe and tassels, again in blue and gold silk. The alcove was a delightful sanctuary that gave a special character to the lady's bedroom. In more modest households, instead of silk there would be *toile de Jouy* and white cotton curtains.

The bedding generally consisted of a horsehair base, two wool mattresses, a feather mattress, a bolster, a square pillow, a woollen blanket and a cotton sheet.

In the homes of the most fashionable ladies, such as that of Mme Récamier in the Chaussée d'Antin, the bedroom was one of the sights to be seen. When the German composer Reichardt stayed in Paris in 1802, it was only natural that he should pay a visit to this queen of fashion: 'To every lady visitor, Mme Récamier would say: "Would you like to see my bedroom?" and she would accompany her arm in arm to her gynaeceum. A cortege of cavaliers would follow close on their heels as they headed for the sanctuary. This lofty room is almost completely surrounded by tall mirrors made of single pieces of glass. Between these, and above the large marquetry doors, one can see white wall panelling with fine brown lines and delicate bronze ornaments. The back wall, facing the windows, is an enormous mirror. And there, its head against the wall, stands the ethereal bed of the goddess of the house: a cloud of chiffon, a white mist! This bed, in the classical style, is decorated with bronze, like the panelling, with as much taste as richness. Around the bed, on a two-tiered base which supports it, are antique-style vases; towards the back are two candelabra, each with eight branches. From the canopy right down to the floor hang

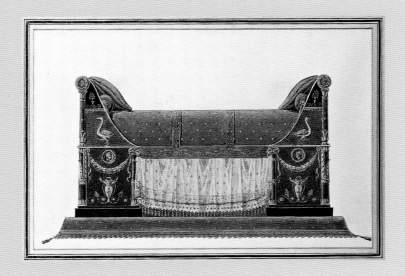

curtains of fine muslin, gracefully draped, protecting the head of the bed. Under these curtains is another drape of purple silk damask, drawn up at the left and right so that one can see the mirror at the back; a wide valance of old-gold-coloured satin, running the length of the cornice, crowns the top of this drapery. It would take too long to describe the bronzes, the paintings that adorn and frame the massive marble fireplace, and to list all the superb items of furniture.' The bed, which was regarded as the most beautiful in Paris, was made of mahogany with gilt bronze decorations; in a completely novel style, it was made in the workshops of the Jacob brothers (see page

143). The architect Berthault, who designed it, introduced the motif of the swan for the very first time, and its success can be gauged from the fact that in 1812 the swan was used on Josephine's bed at Malmaison.

It was a similar story in the house of General Moreau, which was entirely redecorated by Percier and Fontaine in 1801–2. The house was every bit as luxurious that of Mme Récamier, and the bedroom of the general's wife – in a rich harmony of purple and fawn – was on a par with that of the famous beauty. The mahogany bed, now at Fontainebleau, was an important milestone in the history of furniture, as it is believed to have been the first *lit en bateau*, a boat-like design that was to enjoy great success for almost a century.

Beds were generally divided into two types, depending on their position in the room. The *lit de travers* or *lit de milieu* was placed with its long side against the wall, while the *lit de bout* was placed end on, with the headboard against the wall. No matter which position it occupied, there was always a large mirror behind the bed at the back of the alcove. The ready availability of these large mirrors made it possible to install several of them, and thus give more light to the room. The poppy – a flower symbolically linked with sleep and with Morpheus – was often used to decorate the bed, either singly or in garlands or bunches.

Above: The bedroom in the Emperor's private apartments, on the ground floor of the palace of Fontainebleau, retains its bed, which was formerly used by Pope Pius VII at the Tuileries. The beautiful chiné velvet was not installed until 1858, though it had been commissioned in 1811 from the Grand brothers for the Emperor's third salon at Versailles.

Top: Watercolour design for a *lit à flasques*, so named for the two curved panels at each end, which were often decorated with sculpted elements in walnut and gilded bronze, such as swans or sphinxes. This particularly luxurious model was from the studio of Charles Percier, and used amaranth, walnut and gilded bronze.

It had formerly decorated Marie Antoinette's bed at Fontainebleau, and it was to be used again towards the end of the Empire on Josephine's bed at Malmaison (see pages 132–33).

Among the items of furniture that graced these rooms, there was always a bedside cabinet, which was sometimes called a *somno*, from the Latin *somnus*, meaning 'sleep'. The main purpose of this little table was to hold a chamberpot, either round or oval (the latter called a *bourdalou*). The Sèvres factory supplied some very ornate ones for the imperial palaces, often decorated with garlands of ornamental flowers. The bedside cabinets were richly decorated with gilt bronze ornaments representing garlands of poppies, torches, or even a sleeping dog, as on that of General Moreau's wife (see page 33). There was often a washstand near the bed, consisting of a basin resting on a tripod modelled on the famous sphinx tripod from the Temple of Isis at Herculaneum. From 1807 onwards, the cabinet-maker Marcion supplied several of these to the Emperor, all on three- or four-legged stands that ended in lions' feet and were decorated with the heads of naiads. The basins were all made by the imperial factory at Sèvres.

Opposite: As at Fontainebleau, at Compiègne Napoleon decided to use Louis XVI's powder closet for his own bedroom. He entrusted the decoration in 1810 to the studio of Dubois and Redouté; the bed and chairs had been made in 1808 by Jacob-Desmalter. The entire room is draped in crimson damask with a pattern of bees and oak leaves, which is also used to cover the chairs.

Above: The state bedroom in the 'double de Prince' apartment at Compiègne was occupied by, among others, King Jerome of Westphalia and his wife Catherine of Württemberg. The Jacob-Desmalter chairs and the bed, made in 1820 for the Duchesse de Berry's bedroom in the Tuileries, are covered in fawn-coloured gourgouran with purple trimmings.

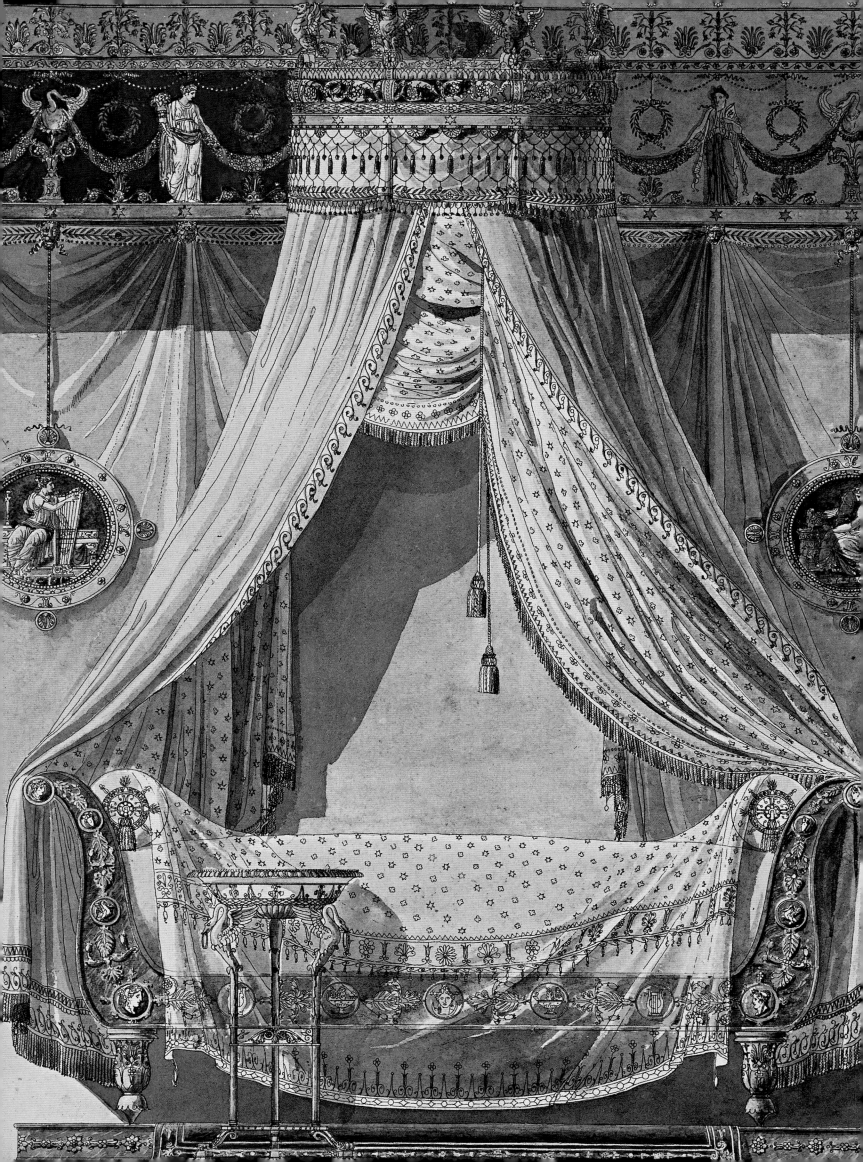

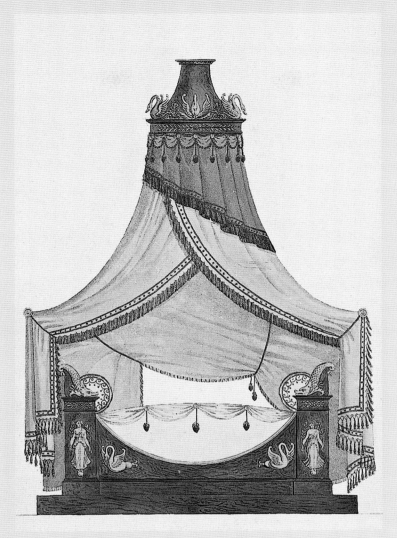

THESE PAGES

Opposite: The bedroom of the wife of General Moreau was one of the most celebrated of the time. It was created around 1802 in her *hôtel* in the rue d'Anjou by Percier and Fontaine. This engraving heightened with watercolour, from their *Recueil de décorations intérieures*, records it precisely; some of the furniture can still be seen in the château at Fontainebleau.

Left: A watercolour design for a *lit à flasques*, based on the famous bed of Juliette Récamier made by the Jacob brothers. Decorative figures echo each other on the head and foot, and the tester is decorated with gilded swans.

PREVIOUS PAGES

Pages 130–31: After her divorce, Josephine decided to replace the decoration of 1800 in her bedroom at Malmaison. The work was carried out in the summer of 1812, during her visit to Milan. Berthault gave the room the form of a sixteen-sided tent, lit by numerous mirrors, and he also designed the bed, which was made by Jacob-Desmalter. There are seven watercolour paintings of flowers on the walls, commissioned from Pierre-Joseph Redouté (1759–1840). The splendour of the decoration, which stands out at Malmaison, is a kind of manifesto by Josephine that, despite her divorce, she intended to remain an Empress.

Pages 132–33: The Empress Josephine's bedroom in her apartment at Compiègne was designed by Berthault in 1808. The divorce prevented her from seeing its completion, and it was the Empress Marie-Louise who eventually used it. As usual, it was the most lavish room in the apartment, and the paintings by Girodet are in keeping with the magnificent mural decorations by the studio of Dubois and Redouté. Textiles also played a crucial role, from muslin with gold embroidery to white corded silk, enhanced by the poppy-red

brocade which covers the walls and is also used for the chairs, by Jacob-Desmalter.

Pages 134–35: Two views of the master bedroom on the first floor of the Hôtel de Beauharnais. It retains its alcove, formed by four columns of carved and gilded mahogany; the bases are decorated with the motif of a winged figure terminating in scrolling arabesques, embracing two swans, all in chased and gilt bronze. The bed is of yew root and speckled mahogany; at either end are mermaids and other motifs in gilt bronze, and in the centre there is a painting under glass of the goddess Flora. All the silks were renewed during restoration work in the 1960s.

Pages 136–37: Two views of the Emperor's bedroom in the private apartments in the Grand Trianon at Versailles. The panelling dates back to the time of Louis XV. Additions included simple furniture of painted wood, which is upholstered in an elegant moiré with lilac star motifs and borders on a lemon yellow ground, commissioned in 1802 from Camille Pernon for Josephine's dressing room at Saint-Cloud. This was supplemented by a washstand and a *somno*, by the cabinetmaker Marcion, and a barometer by Chevallier. The only

note of comparative luxury is provided by the chest of drawers and the mahogany writing desk, in the form of a triumphal arch, supplied by the furniture dealer Baudoin in 1809 but with bronze ornaments made around 1785.

Pages 138–39: The master bedroom in the Hôtel Bourrienne is situated on the ground floor, looking out on the garden and adjoining the drawing room. This extraordinary room has a curved alcove which holds the bed. The panels on the walls have such lavish painted decoration that Josephine, when paying a visit to Mme de Bourrienne, is said to have cried: 'My god, this is more beautiful than the First Consul's house!'

Page 140: A counterpane with a richly embroidered 'J' surmounted by the imperial crown, typical of the bedlinen to be found at Malmaison. There were other counterpanes of *toile de Jouy*, dimity and cotton twill.

Page 141: Josephine had two bedrooms at Malmaison. Her *grande chambre* contained numerous chairs for visitors, whereas this one, known as the *chambre ordinaire*, which she preferred, had simple mahogany furniture covered with white silk embroidered in gold and with gold fringe.

Wallpaper

Wallpaper as we know it began with single sheets of coloured or printed paper known in France as *dominos* or *papiers de tapisserie*. Decorated with repeating motifs, these were difficult to use because getting all the edges to match when filling a wall was a long and painstaking task. It was the English who first had the idea of arranging the motifs end to end in rolls, some 10 metres (30 ft) in length: these had a plain coloured background, on which the patterns were either stencilled or printed. The technique was introduced into France in the middle of the 18th century, and grew rapidly in popularity thanks to the genius of Jean-Baptiste Réveillon, who on the eve of the

Revolution was at the head of a company employing more than three hundred people; his firm's decorative panel papers were a huge success. The late 18th and early 19th centuries saw a flowering of arabesque repeat patterns, with scenes often arranged one above the other, and papers could be applied not only to the walls but also to the ceilings of rooms to create a complete ensemble. The use of papers in dados and as borders became widespread. Some designs imitated the flower and leaf motifs used in silk, in order to offer a cheaper alternative; others gave the illusion of drapes hanging from curtain rails, or replicated lace, tartan, or striped fabrics. With the arrival of the Empire, the

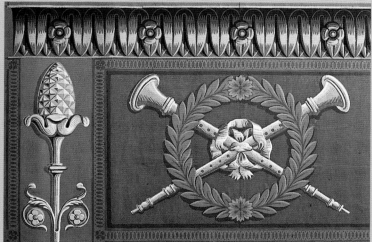

Above, left and right: A wallpaper with repeating motifs inspired by textile designs, and a dado paper, from *Décors et leurs bordures* published by the Parisian manufacturer Jacquemart around 1810. It was popular in the Empire period to divide the wall into an upper zone of panels covered in small motifs and accentuated by vertical pilasters, and a richly decorated border or frieze.

Opposite: This dolphin frieze gave its name to a set of wallpapers produced in 1810–12 by the firm of Zuber in Alsace. The motif is distinctive, but the rest of the paper was standard for the time, using repeat motifs inspired by textiles (the manufacturer called it satin).

Top, left and right: It is not known who printed this wallpaper with gold motifs and an ermine border, but the allegorical figure was taken from Percier and Fontaine's *Recueil de décorations intérieures*.

Above: These wallpaper samples are both by Joseph Dufour (1754–1827): the one with palmettes was printed in 1802 at Mâcon by Dufour Frères et Cie, while the green striped design was produced in 1808 by the firm of Joseph Dufour, by then in Paris. Once again we see the Empire period's love of textile effects.

imaginative arabesque designs gave way to classical motifs, such as spears, helmets, wreaths, swords, banners, shields and winged victories. The freedom given by the new techniques allowed the designers unlimited scope for their imaginations: they could put together violently clashing combinations of colours, and counterfeit marble, architectural detailing and scenes from Antiquity. The richness of the colours gave these wallpapers an extraordinary three-dimensionality and shimmer. Some papers required no less than eighty stages of printing with different blocks, and could rival the finest paintings, velvets and silks, although between eleven and twenty-seven colours were generally enough to reproduce the effect of lace, moiré or drapery. It was not until after 1830 that printing by roller, already used for textiles, began to be used for wallpaper, thus greatly increasing the speed of production.

Jean Houël wrote about this fashion phenomenon in the *Journal du Lycée des Arts* (1795): 'For appearance, cleanliness, freshness and elegance, these papers are to be preferred to the rich fabrics of yesteryear; they provide no home for insects, and if they are varnished, they retain the brightness and charm of their colours for a long time; furthermore, they can very easily be changed, and since we can thus afford to refurbish our sanctuaries, clean them more often, and render them livelier and more pleasant,

these wallpapers help to make life more interesting and so deserve to be regarded as a vital product of industry.'

Indeed, the number of wallpaper factories in Paris increased by leaps and bounds, from fifty in 1789 to sixty-seven in 1803 and ninety-six in 1811. Two associates of Réveillon, Jacquemart and Bénard, succeeded him after the Revolution and gave new impetus to the industry: they supplied wallpaper to most of the imperial palaces – Fontainebleau, Compiègne, Rambouillet and Saint-Cloud – though the papers were only used to decorate anterooms, stairwells and secondary apartments, as well as cupboard interiors, screens, overdoors and firescreens. There was no question of using them in the reception rooms, on which Napoleon himself kept a close eye. One day, when supervising the work of decoration at Fontainebleau, he is said to have discovered to his amazement some Jacquemart wallpapers which at first he had taken for silk. Furious, he is reputed to have declared: 'I think I have the means to pay for the real thing!' The bourgeoisie followed the trend, thus endowing their walls with the luxury of the velvets and silks that were otherwise unavailable to them. The object was to deceive the observer's eye and provide the best possible imitation of stucco and silk.

Technical developments also began to allow the creation of panoramic papers. Taking up the concept of the rotundas

Above: Both the iconography and the colour place this dado in the Empire period. Its origin and date are unknown, but the motifs used in its decoration recall the best work of designers in Paris and Lyons.

built in 1799 in the boulevard Montmartre, cylindrical buildings in which one could admire huge circular paintings depicting, for example, a view of Paris or the siege of Toulon, panoramic wallpaper now took over the walls of the salons, as tapestries had once done, with scenes that could extend over 15 metres (50 ft) in length. Two factories in particular cornered this market: that of Jean Zuber, at Rixheim in Alsace, and that of Joseph Dufour in Mâcon. The role of the designer was crucial to the success of firms of this kind. Zuber initially employed the painter Joseph-Laurent Malaine, who created designs of flower baskets and vases, obliging the printers to work wonders in order to reproduce the great variety of colours. But it was Antoine-Pierre Mongin who was responsible for the firm's fame in the field of panoramic papers. His first success was 'Les Jardins de Bagatelle' – probably the first panoramic paper, printed in 1795–1802. He repeated the triumph in 1804 with 'Les Vues de Suisse', a sixteen-sheet set, followed in 1806 by 'L'Hindoustan', in 1811 by 'L'Arcadie', and in 1814 by 'La Grande Helvétie'.

The rival company, Dufour, employed the designer Jean-Gabriel Charvet, who created 'Les Sauvages de la Mer Pacifique' in 1804, based on the voyages of Captain Cook; Xavier Mader designed 'Les Portiques d'Athènes' (1808), and the son of the famous painter Fragonard, Alexandre-

Top: This wide border was printed by Jacquemart & Bénard in Paris in 1804. The identical paper appears in a handsome room in a château in Normandy, where it accompanies a fictive hanging with colonnettes, topped by swags of fabric and a band with plant motifs just below the ceiling.

Above: This frieze with its motifs of antique ceramics can in all probability be attributed to the Lyons firm of Dusserre et Cie, directed by Camille Pernon, for which the painter Pierre Révoil produced wallpaper designs, because an identical border was found in the archives of Tassinari et Chatel, successors of Pernon.

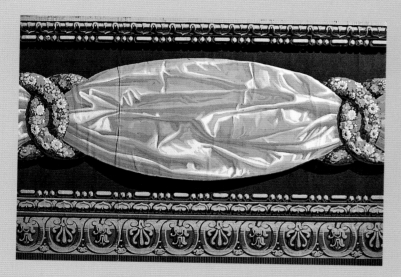

Évariste, designed a series based on the months of the year in 1808. But the panorama that sealed Dufour's success was 'The Tale of Cupid and Psyche', in twelve scenes, inspired by La Fontaine's retelling of the story. Begun in 1814 and put on the market in 1816, this series was the work of two artists, Louis Lafitte and Merry-Joseph Blondel. Printed in grisaille, it enjoyed an enormous popularity, and examples could be found as far afield as Bavaria, Sweden, and the shores of the Baltic; the success even extended into the 20th century when the paper was revived by the firm of Follot.

French wallpaper enjoyed great prestige overseas, and the major firms had representatives all over Europe as well as in the Americas. More than 120 examples of French panoramic wallpapers were sold to the United States, where they could be found in places stretching from the plantations of Louisiana to the houses of Natchez, Mississippi.

Top: This frieze, from the 1810–12 catalogue of the Paris firm of Joseph Dufour, was intended to be placed at the top of the wall. It was designed to accompany the *trompe-l'oeil* drapery shown on page 159, using the same multicoloured floral garlands and pleats, but with the addition of gilt bronze border motifs.

Above: This arched frieze is part of a wallpaper scheme that also includes a paper with repeating motifs and a lower border, designed to be hung above a dado. The printing technique used, known as *linon batiste*, was patented by Jacquemart & Bénard in 1802. The net and tassels in the arch are a further allusion to the world of textiles.

PREVIOUS PAGES
Pages 150–51: An allegorical figure of the city of Lyons decorates this overdoor in grisaille. The pair of lions and personification of the city are very close to those in a plaster of 1805–10 by Ennemond-Alexandre Petitot called *La Concorde*.

Pages 152–53: The columns framing this paper in a house in Barjols, in the Var region of France, were designed by the predecessors of Zuber, Hartmann Risler, in 1795–96, but the maker of the main paper, with its drapery on a mint-green ground, scattered with flowers enhanced with mica spangles, is unknown. It may be by Jacquemart in Paris, which presented wallpapers 'incorporating transparent spangles' at the 1806 Exhibition of the Products of French Industry, or one of the firms in Lyons, or Zuber.

Pages 154–55: Shortly after the firm's move to Paris, Joseph Dufour called on the talents of the young Alexandre-Evariste Fragonard, who designed a series of papers based on the months of the year. Two versions were offered by the firm in 1808 – in grisaille with brown highlights, and in ochre on a blue ground. The Musée des Arts Décoratifs in Paris has samples of both: *September* and *October* (seen here), *November*, *December* and *May* in grisaille, and *February*, *April*, *July* and *August* in ochre.

Pages 156–157: 'Les Sauvages de la Mer Pacifique', also known as 'The Voyages of Captain Cook', was produced by Dufour Frères et Cie in 1804, and presented at the Exhibition of the Products of French Industry in 1806. It was described as 'a decorative painting in wallpaper, based on the discoveries of Captains Cook and de la Pérouze and other travellers, forming a finely shaded landscape, executed in twenty panels of paper, measuring 20 inches in length by 90 inches in height'.

The paper, with its non-repeating panels, was advertised by Moiroux of Mâcon as allowing the creation of 'an endless tableau, because the two ends may be joined to form a sort of panorama to be cut into twenty-inch lengths, which can be used in isolation or in groups of two, three, four, five, six, seven, eight, ten, twelve or more, according to the wishes of the owner or the arrangement of the apartments that are to be decorated'.

At the 1806 exhibition, it was described as follows: 'M. Joseph Dufour, of Mâcon, already famed for his wallpaper factory, has produced a new series of papers, of which the subjects drawn from the voyages of Captain Cook are perhaps the most curious

products of this type so far. No trouble, no care, no financial sacrifice could discourage M. Dufour. There were endless difficulties to overcome; everything had to be thought out anew; finally he reached his goal, and the point where he can gather the fruit of his long labours.'

The annotated design preserved in the Musée des Beaux-Arts in Lyons, and the account of the twenty panels that make up the complete design by Jean-Gabriel Charvet (1750–1829), make it possible to identify the tribal peoples depicted in the section illustrated here:

'Nos. XV and XVI. Inhabitants of Tongatabo, the largest of the Friendly Islands [Tonga], 21° S, 182° W.
No. XVII. Inhabitants of Santa Cristina, the most populated of the Marquesas Islands.
No. XVIII. Inhabitants of the Marquesas Islands, 9° S, 138° W. Discovered by Minda [*sic*] in 1595, and visited in 1773 by Captain Cook.
No. XIX. Inhabitants of Easter Island, 27° S, 109° W. Discovered by Davis in 1686. Captain Cook stopped there on his second voyage, in 1773.
No. XX. Inhabitants of Palau, 7° N, 135° W.'

The paper, from the Banque Indosuez, includes an additional panel at the far right, created by a restorer, who looked for inspiration to Dufour's panorama 'Les Incas' of 1818.

THESE PAGES
Opposite: This paper with a Grecian vase motif was designed by Joseph-Laurent Malaine and printed in 1802 by Zuber. Malaine, who worked as a flower painter for the Manufacture des Gobelins, here displays his talent for still life; but – either out of personal taste or because he was required to by Zuber – he submitted to the fashion of the day in including antique motifs and three-dimensional putti playing musical instruments.

Right: This satin curtain, held back by garlands of coloured flowers, was designed to go with the border shown on page 149. Both were printed by Joseph Dufour in 1810–12, and show the love of imitation textiles in the wallpapers of this period. The painstaking portrayal of the fabric and the delicate floral motifs point to Lyons as the origin of the designs.

CAPTIONS IN THIS CHAPTER BY Véronique Bruignac-La Hougue

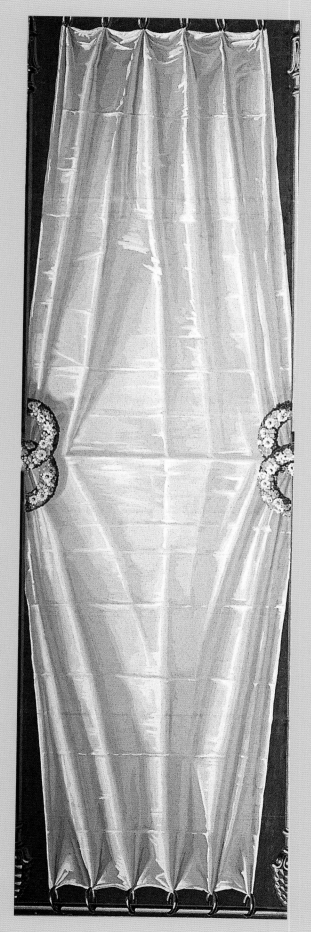

Bathrooms and dressing rooms

At the beginning of the 18th century, rooms specially set aside for bathing were rare; people were highly suspicious of contact between water and body, believing that it could infiltrate the organs and weaken them. Water was therefore used only to wash the face and hands, and that purpose was amply served by the jugs and basins kept in the bedroom, which could be made of anything from rich Sèvres porcelain to simple pipeclay. Although Louis XV had a bathroom installed at Versailles in 1723, the idea did not catch on until the end of the century, and even then Marie Antoinette had to use two baths – one to wash herself and one to rinse herself – as the single bathtub was a rarity. In 1801, a survey of sixty-six private residences built since 1770 mentions only twenty bathrooms: a ratio of not even one in three. Most people had to make do with public baths. A few wealthier homes had a bathtub of their own, which was hidden away when not in use. Aside from the bathrooms installed for the sovereigns in their palaces, very few private individuals had the means to enjoy either a bathroom or the dressing room that would normally adjoin it. These two rooms had very different functions, the former being for bathing itself, and the latter for preparation. There were no precise rules, however, and sometimes the roles could merge. In her apartment at the Tuileries, Josephine had a room which the inventory called a *toilette* (dressing room) or *boudoir*, and this contained no less than twenty chairs, a dressing table and a cheval mirror. Next to it, the bathroom contained a galvanized copper bath, six chairs and a bookshelf. At Fontainebleau, the bath was sunk into the floor and covered with a platform that supported a couch, so that the bathroom could be changed into a boudoir. The same principle was used at Compiègne: in the Empress's boudoir, the bath was concealed beneath upholstery in a recess opposite the fireplace.

Few of these luxurious bathrooms have survived. Apart from those in the Hôtel de Beauharnais and Hôtel Bourrienne, there is one in the palace at Rambouillet, whose lavish Pompeian decor earned a sharp rebuke for the architect from Napoleon, who dismissed 'M. Famin's little decorations'. In the Emperor's other palaces, the dominant characteristic of these rooms was simplicity: chairs covered with white striped dimity and bath curtains of muslin at the Grand Trianon and Fontainebleau, furniture in plane wood at Compiègne. It was the same in private homes, where chairs and walls were generally covered with plain textiles – percale, cotton, dimity, nankeen – often pleated and held back with pegs, all finished off with muslin. The bath itself was sometimes decorated on the outside with painted motifs, and it was usually placed in an alcove and covered with a canopy hung with curtains of muslin or some other fabric.

Left: Watercolour design for a bathroom, by an unknown artist.

Opposite: In this self-portrait, the artist Constance Mayer (1774–1821) depicts herself wearing a gown known as a *toilette du matin*, which was fashionable at the beginning of the Consulate period: a white chiffon dress with high waist and bare arms. Napoleon disapproved of this style of dress, deeming it to be indecent.

Right: This crystal ewer and basin were made in the Montcenis factory at Le Creusot. The ewer, an exceptional piece, is in the form of a Greek vase and is an outstanding example of engraving on glass. On the body is a procession of the nine Muses towards the helmeted figure of the goddess Minerva, a composition based on an engraving by Laurent Guyot after a drawing by the sculptor Moitte.

In contrast to the previous century, baths were no longer made of wood lined with lead, but of red copper galvanized on the inside. In the 1770s, the first sheet metal baths had made their appearance, covered with enamel that made them more pleasant to touch; others were made of zinc. Baths of marble or other hard stone were too cold, and gradually went out of fashion. There was a wide variety of shapes: some were like a couch, while others allowed you to sit in a wicker seat like an armchair; the latter gave rise to the hip bath, which took up less space as it was more compact (and which became famous as a result of Marat's assassination by Charlotte Corday). Hardly any baths were now made of wood except those of the less well off or those that were rented out and carried to people's houses; ordinary people did not always have the means to hire a cloth to hang on the walls of the tub. In spite of all this progress, there were only 250 public baths in Paris in 1780, and even by 1850 the 950,000 inhabitants of the capital had only taken 2,166,320 baths between them – an average of 2.23 baths per person per year!

The dressing room was always situated next to the bedroom. It had to be large enough to accommodate the wardrobes containing all the necessary requisites: gowns, undergarments, and boxes for storing more delicate accessories. Only the larger houses had a special room for all the finery, with oak cupboards, coat racks and sliding drawers. During the day the dressing room served to house things used at night, such as bedside cabinets, pillows and night lights. It might also contain a marble or sandstone fountain with a filter, in which to store water and, more importantly, to get rid of any silt. If there was no separate room for such objects, the dressing room could also contain the lavatory, bidet and bowl for washing one's feet.

The Scotsman John Pinkerton lauded the virtues of the public baths of Paris, saying that 'Parisian bathtubs of galvanized copper, which incidentally are more numerous than they are at home, reduce the risk of catching cold because they are installed in confined spaces and are also more in keeping with the rules of propriety. For little more than a shilling, customers of both sexes can enjoy the delights of a hot or cold bath, including service and accessories.'

Right: This engraving by Antoine Cardon after a painting by Jean-Baptiste Mallet shows a woman at her toilet. She gazes at herself in an oval cheval glass, while her cashmere shawl lies carelessly thrown over a chair.

Opposite, left: For the Emperor's various palaces the cabinetmaker Pierre-Benoît Marcion supplied ten washstands, each with three or four legs topped with the heads of naiads. This one, for Napoleon's bedroom at Compiègne, has a basin of Sèvres porcelain known as the 'Imperial Basin'; it is is alone among Napoleon's basins in having gold decoration on a white, rather than a blue or green, ground.

Opposite, centre: The Emperor's commode at Compiègne is virtually identical to that at the Grand Trianon, supplied by Jacob-Desmalter. A purely functional piece, it appears very simple apart from the gilt bronze feet in the form of lions' paws. The top opens on hinges, revealing a seat of green silk velvet with gold trimmings. The bowl is of white porcelain.

The Rev. Mr Hughes, travelling through the western provinces, was shocked by the lack of modern conveniences: 'It is disheartening to find that there is not a single water closet or anything like one in the magnificent French houses, where one dines from dishes of solid silver.' Although they did make a very tentative appearance at the end of the 18th century, water closets developed very slowly, and were regarded as extremely peculiar by those who did not use them. At Versailles from 1770 onwards, Mme du Barry had an English-style flush toilet, but Napoleon and Josephine were content to use a simple mahogany commode with a velvet seat concealing a porcelain basin that had to be emptied at regular intervals. Generally the French preferred chamberpots. The bidet, which made its appearance at the beginning of the 18th century, gradually became more widespread, and was almost always made of Rouen earthenware, except for the one supplied in 1812 to the Empress Josephine by the imperial factory at Sèvres – in white porcelain richly decorated with gold mosaic, beads and fillets.

As far as personal hygiene was concerned, Napoleon was quite exceptional. He was meticulous in his devotion to cleanliness, and developed something akin to a passion for hot baths, often spending more than an hour revelling in the steamy atmosphere. Then he would regularly have his beard shaved – he would rarely allow it to grow for more than a week – after which he would wash his hands and face, dip his head into the basin, and give his teeth a good brushing. Finally, after carefully cutting his nails, he would have himself briskly scrubbed all over with eau de cologne, telling his valet: 'Harder, harder! As if I were a donkey!' Josephine took a bath every day, and wherever she went, she would take with her kettles, basins and bowls – all of them in silver – for washing her feet.

La Toilette

Le Bon Genre, N° 5.

Rue Montmartre N° 40.

THESE PAGES

Left: The satirical revue *Le Bon Genre*, subtitled 'Observation of the Manners and Customs of Paris', published from 1813 onwards, included several illustrations of ladies at their toilette. Like the famous *Journal des Modes*, its editor was the celebrated Pierre La Mésangère (1761–1831).

Below: A gouache of 1812, the artist of which is unknown, shows a young man dressing, admiring himself in a cheval glass.

Opposite: The definitive piece of gentleman's furniture, the shaving stand enabled men to shave while standing up; for this purpose, it was equipped with a mirror. It was an expensive item which only the very rich could afford. The instruments on particular stand – shaving dish, razor, shaving brush, toothbrush – belonged to General Brayer, whose daughter later married Marchand, the Emperor's valet on St Helena. Dressing cases supplied by Biennais or Maire contained at least two razors, a shaving brush and a bowl.

PREVIOUS PAGES

Pages 166–67: The bathroom of the Empress's private apartment at Fontainebleau. At the back of the room a couch stands on a retractable platform covering the bath, sunk into the floor, so the room could be transformed into a salon. The couch is of gilded wood, as are the four gondola-shaped armchairs designed by Percier, the two side chairs, and the screen – all upholstered with sky-blue gourgouran. The cheval glass and the dressing table with adjustable mirror, set between candelabra surmounted by winged victories, and richly decorated with gilt bronze, were made by Thomire in 1809.

Page 168: In *La Toilette*, engraved after a work traditionally attributed to Prud'hon, a woman leans against her dressing table as her maid helps her to dress.

Page 169: On the Empress Josephine's dressing table of yew – probably supplied by the Jacob brothers around 1800 for her boudoir at the Tuileries – are various objects that once belonged to her, including a tortoiseshell comb, a watch and a small box of perfumes. On the floor is a pair of her fur boots, and on the back of the chair is a chiffon shawl with gold stripes.

Pages 170–71: Hoping to please the Emperor, the architect of Rambouillet, Auguste-Pierre Famin (1776–1859), designed a bathroom of which the decoration included fourteen medallions

containing views of Italy and of the imperial palaces, painted in 1809–10 by Jean Vasserot (see also pages 190, 191). The bath is of galvanized copper. The furniture was covered with white dimity. The overall effect was completely contrary to Napoleon's preference for simplicity, and he declared himself unhappy with 'M. Farnin's little decorations'.

Page 172: In *Le Bain*, an engraving by Girard after a painting by Jean-Baptiste Mallet, the bath is imaginatively shown as made of glass.

Page 173: Napoleon's bath at Compiègne is of stone, lined with copper.

Pages 174–75: The Empress Josephine's magnificent *nécessaire*, shown at the Exhibition of the Products of French Industry in 1806, was created by the cabinetmaker Félix Rémond (1779–after 1841). Intended for her boudoir in the Tuileries, it contained forty-four pieces in silver gilt, mother-of-pearl, tortoiseshell, porcelain and crystal, for toilet, sewing, embroidery and writing. Every piece bears Josephine's monogram; silver items have the mark of Pierre Leplain, who made them in 1803. The remarkable decoration design in cut steel is by Reynard Schey, a specialist in the technique, which is reminiscent of work from the Russian town of Tula. In the centre is a miniature portrait of Napoleon, signed by Vigneux, a pupil of

Isabey. After the divorce, the case was sent to Malmaison, and it was sold after Josephine's death. Napoleon III bought it back for the first museum he set up at Malmaison during the Second Empire, thus returning it to its former home in the Empress's apartments.

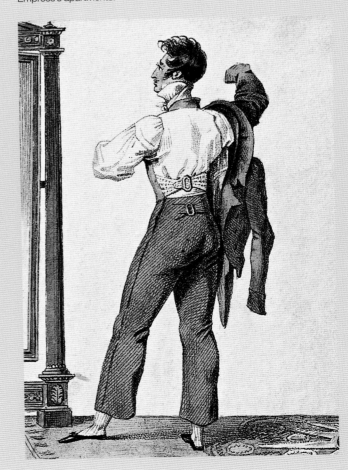

Painted decoration

Because of its high cost, painted decoration was only to be found in imperial palaces and great houses. Sometimes real paintings would be set into panelling, as at Compiègne, where the famous painter Anne-Louis Girodet created a whole series of works for the walls and ceilings of the Emperor and Empress's apartments – but this was exceptional. For the most part, studios were called upon to carry out designs by architects, of whom the best-known were Percier and Fontaine.

Percier and Fontaine's first commission, in 1799, was to decorate the small boudoir of the *hôtel* of Bernard-François de Chauvelin in the rue Chantereine, which Josephine saw before commissioning them to design Malmaison. That boudoir encapsulated the basic decorative repertoire that was to become typical of the age: helmets set within laurel wreaths, walls divided by slender colonnettes topped by swans, putti and peacocks, all executed in bold colours. Most of the subjects were taken from Antiquity, and the two architects drew copiously on the notes and sketches they had made during their visits to Rome, combining the arabesque style favoured under Louis XVI with the painting of the ancient world. The great skill of the decorative painters enabled them to create imitations of porphyry, granite and other hardstones. Unlike Italian wall paintings, which favoured the fresco technique, these were painted in oil, with great care and precise attention to detail. Only the backgrounds were sometimes painted in fresco, as in the library ceiling at Malmaison.

Sadly, very few of these interiors have survived. The *hôtels* of Récamier and Moreau, Isabey and Ouvrard were all demolished, and from the period of the Consulate there remain only the painted decoration of Malmaison, dating from 1800, and of the Hôtel Bourrienne in the rue d'Hauteville, begun in 1801. At Malmaison, Percier produced all the designs himself, and they were executed by several painters, including Moench (known as Munich), who also worked at Fontainebleau, and Protain, who belonged to the painting workshop at the Opéra. The most significant decorating firm of the Empire period was founded by Antoine-Ferdinand Redouté, the brother of the famous flower painter, in association with Étienne Dubois. From 1805 onwards, they worked under the supervision of the architect Berthault on the decorative paintings at Malmaison and then at Compiègne. Another notable architect was Étienne-Chérubin Leconte, who designed the decorations for the reception rooms of the Hôtel Bourrienne.

Left: The library at Malmaison: an engraving heightened in watercolour, from Percier and Fontaine's *Recueil de décorations intérieures*.

Opposite: The doors of the Salon des Saisons in the Hôtel de Beauharnais display eight of the nine Muses: Terpsichore, the muse of dance, and Thalia, the muse of comedy, are seen here; other doors pair Calliope and Euterpe, Erato and Polyhymnia, and Clio and Melpomene.

THESE PAGES

Left: Detail of the frieze in the Emperor's bathroom in the château of Rambouillet.

Left, below: The doors of the state bedroom in the Hôtel de Beauharnais are made of polished wood, in the natural shades of mahogany, walnut and oak. In the centre of each door is a painted putto against a black ground. One carries a torch, another flowers, and a third plays a tambourine. The one seen here is firing an arrow of love.

Opposite: The ceiling of the bathroom at Rambouillet uses marine motifs appropriate to its watery purpose. The overall rectangular shape contains three lozenges, of which one depicts a sea horse and another a monster with Neptune's trident.

PREVIOUS PAGES

Pages 180–81: The general scheme of the ceiling of the library at Malmaison was provided by Percier. In the centre are Minerva and Apollo, flanked by personifications of Music and War. The rest of the ceiling features twelve medallions with the heads of famous ancient and modern authors, probably painted by Louis Lafitte. In pairs, facing one another, are Virgil and Homer, Voltaire and Dante, Ovid and Ossian, Polybius and Xenophon, Herodotus and Socrates, and Cicero and the Abbé Raynal. From Fontaine's diary, we know that the whole ceiling was painted in just ten days, in September 1800.

Pages 182–83: Like all the decorative paintings in the Emperor's bathroom at Rambouillet, the lunette above the bath is by Pierre-François Godard. Some of the less obtrusive Napoleonic emblems, such as the swarm of bees leaving the golden hive, were retained; fleurs-de-lis and the 'L' monogram of Louis XVIII were added in the Restoration period.

Page 184: In the the music room at the Hôtel de Beauharnais, below figures of four Muses – Urania, Terpsichore, Euterpe and Calliope – is an elegant frieze of swans whose bodies end in foliated scrolls, connected by garlands of flowers. The artist is unfortunately unknown.

Page 185: The Empress Josephine's bedroom at Compiègne was decorated to Berthault's design from 1808 to mid-1809 by the studio of Dubois and Redouté. It is articulated by a series of pilasters painted with scrolls and grotesques, showing Josephine's love of the arabesque style.

Pages 186–87: The painter of the main bedroom in the Hôtel Bourrienne is unknown, but the decorative vocabulary suggests the early years of the 19th century. The figures of Cupid and Psyche are surrounded by panels featuring birds perched on stems with palmettes and stylized flowers.

Page 188: The panels on the bedroom walls of the Hôtel Bourrienne, with as a centrepiece a head in a medallion, echo the decorative motifs of the ceiling, with vases of flowers, swans, fluttering butterflies, and brilliantly coloured birds, all framed within palmettes and stylized flower stems.

Page 189: The doors of the *salon de compagnie* in the Hôtel Bourrienne have semicircular tympana of late Louis XVI type, which may well date from the original period of construction, 1787–90. However, the decorative paintings of candelabra on the doors must be part of the redecoration begun for Bourrienne in 1801.

Studies and libraries

The study was the gentleman's room par excellence, and it was usually associated with the library. In private houses in the 18th century, you might find books anywhere, including the bedroom, the anteroom, and sometimes even the kitchen. This was not always due to lack of space, but rather to the fact that in those days it was simply not common practice to keep books in a specific place. It was different at Versailles, however, where Louis XV had a library installed in his private apartments in 1728. Later, Louis XVI, Marie Antoinette and Mme du Barry all had libraries in their apartments.

There were still very few libraries in private houses in the Empire period. Most people kept books in bookcases, which were preferable to shelves fixed to the walls because they could be moved. The sculptor Moitte, who had a very fine apartment on the quai Malaquais, had three bookcases in the drawing room, and a mahogany writing desk and chair in his bedroom. For the leisured classes, the study needed to be a serious, even austere, room. There one would find nothing but the bare necessities – a bookcase, a secretaire, a desk, a clock, and a number of chairs, usually of mahogany, covered with clean, hard-wearing cloth or leather. There might also be a sofa that could be used as a bed.

The customs of the elite were just as varied. In the Élysée Palace, Murat had a room on the first floor made into a library, with bookcases on three of the walls. Prince Eugène, on the other hand, was content with two huge, two-piece bookcases in the anteroom on the ground floor, opening out to the garden (they are still there today). His sister, Queen Hortense, had a large bookcase in her boudoir in the house in the rue Cerutti (it is now in the Napoleonmuseum at Schloss Arenenberg in Switzerland). Marshals Soult, Berthier and Lannes all set aside a room in their Paris houses for a library (Ney did not have one). In the château of Maisons-Laffitte, Lannes had two monumental bookcases installed with glazed doors in the lower part and colonnettes in the upper part (now in the Bibliothèque Marmottan at Boulogne-Billancourt).

It was the Emperor, however, who was responsible for the best examples of this type of room. It is well known that Napoleon could not do without his books. A creature of habit, in each of his residences he had a library built, which also served as a study. When he was still only a general, he had already adorned his study in the house in the rue de la Victoire with five mahogany bookcases that had mirrored doors and richly chased gilt bronze decorations. He was so fond of them that he had them taken to Rambouillet in 1806. The earliest of his libraries to survive is the one at Malmaison. Installed in the summer of 1800, it is intact, with a painted ceiling containing figures of Apollo and

Opposite: *Portrait of a Man sealing a Letter*, by Constance-Marie Charpentier. It was customary to seal the letter itself or the envelope with wax, impressed with a seal engraved with one's initials. Sealing wax was often sold in small round pieces, known as *pains à cacheter*. (This portrait is a companion piece to the *Portrait of a Woman drinking Coffee* reproduced on page 63.)

Previous pages: For his study in the Tuileries, the First Consul did not wish to use a roll-top desk that would block his view, and he asked the Jacob brothers to design a low desk that would allow him to leave his work without having to clear the papers away. They came up with this *bureau mécanique*, with a top like a kind of rectangular box with a lid that slid on runners, so that the desk could be closed without rearranging the documents inside.

Minerva, surrounded by medallions depicting great writers from Homer to the Abbé Raynal, who had died only four years earlier (see pages 180–81). We know that in 1814 it held between 4,500 and 5,000 books.

Paradoxically, the Tuileries library contained the smallest number of books. At the time of the Consulate, Napoleon had planned to install sixteen bookcases in the palace to hold 10,000 volumes, but he quickly gave up the idea because he found it easy enough to have any books he wanted brought from the imperial library storehouse in the rue du Bac, which was just across the Seine. The room that became the library is small – barely 30 m² (320 sq. ft) – and had wall space for only two bookcases at right angles to each other for keeping important documents, and a table in the window bay for the use of his private secretary – first Bourrienne and later Méneval. The centre of the room was taken up by the magnificent *bureau mécanique* which Napoleon himself devised and which was made for him by the Jacob brothers. It is 2.3 metres (7½ ft) long, and looks like a flat desk, surmounted by a kind of shallow box with a lid sliding on runners, which allowed it to be closed without any need to clear the desktop (this desk is now in the museum at Malmaison). He was so pleased with it that he had copies made for his other residences, and examples are still to be seen at Fontainebleau and Compiègne. Murat also

had versions made for the Elysée Palace and Caserta, and in England the Prince Regent, later to become George IV, had one in his London home.

This type of 'box' desk remained exceptional. Far more common was the *bureau plat*, which was usually double-sided. Sometimes instead there was a roll-top desk or *bureau à cylindre*, which was also popular; desks in this style tended to be simplified versions of Louis XV's famous roll-top desk, designed by Oeben in 1769 and completed by Riesener. Marquetry was replaced by plain wood, usually mahogany, which enhanced the architectural feel of this item of Empire furniture. Drop-leaf secretaires were mainly placed in bedrooms: they rarely served for writing, since they were much less convenient than a flat desk. The inside of the leaf would be covered in leather, like the top of a writing desk, and secretaires were often decorated with gilt bronze and accompanied by a commode in a matching design.

The Emperor liked to have his library close to his council chamber and his *cabinet topographique* (map room), but sometimes the layout of a building would not allow this. Nevertheless, the architects would do their best to get the two rooms as close together as possible. At the imperial palace in Strasbourg, for example, the old episcopal library became the *cabinet topographique* while still serving as a library; the seven cabinets that had been installed there

Left: This inkwell, with a crowned 'J', was commissioned by the Empress Josephine from the porcelain factory of Dihl and Guérhard as a present for Nicolas-Rodolphe de Watteville, Landammann (chief official) of Switzerland and Avoyer (chief magistrate) of the canton of Berne.

seventy years earlier were simply given an additional 'N' in gilt bronze. At the Grand Trianon, the *cabinet topographique* also doubled as a library. At Saint-Cloud, after the Consulate, Napoleon had some large mahogany bookcases put in his study, and these were later sent to Fontainebleau, where from 1804 onwards they became part of his library on the ground floor. He did the same at Compiègne, where in 1808 the Jacob brothers built magnificent bookcases in mahogany and gilded wood. When the Emperor wanted a library installed at Laeken, he gave precise details: 'I want my study to be in the middle of a library and, as at Saint-Cloud and Malmaison, on the same level as the garden.'

Altogether, these imperial libraries contained some 60,000 books. The shelving everywhere followed the system established at Malmaison, so that the Emperor could easily find what he was looking for. In order to show which

books came from where, each volume bore the name of the palace it belonged to.

Napoleon was not a bibliophile, but he was certainly an avid reader. As far as he was concerned, the sole purpose of a book was its usefulness: he was only interested in the content, and if he did not like it, he would not hesitate to throw the book on the fire or out of his carriage door. He read quickly, and he read a lot, though he rarely finished works he had started. During his military campaigns, he always took hundreds of books with him, and he gave some thought to setting up a mobile library of a thousand volumes, planning the subject categories himself: poetry and history, historical memoirs, novels, religion, epic literature, and theatre. The project sadly never saw the light of day. He maintained his taste for books right through to the end of his life, and on St Helena he had a collection of more than 3,500 volumes, all stored in a single room at Longwood House.

Meubles et Objets de Goût.

Secretaire - Bibliothèque.

Left: Design for a drop-leaf secretaire with bookcases, from *Meubles et objects de goût*, a journal published between 1802 and 1835 by Pierre La Mésangère, with 755 colour plates.

PREVIOUS PAGES

Pages 198–99: Scarcely had he arrived at Malmaison than the First Consul asked Percier and Fontaine to design a workspace on the ground floor which, most importantly, would contain a library. The architects decided to put it in the south wing, turning several smaller rooms – including some on the mezzanine – into one large space as a counterpart to the music salon. However, they came up against a major problem: the flues of the kitchen fireplace, directly below, passed through the room and could not be moved. The architects came up with the ingenious idea of concealing them behind mirrors between mahogany columns supporting an arch. The result was criticized by Napoleon as looking like a 'church sacristy'.

Page 200: The Emperor's library at Compiègne was designed by Berthault in 1808, and the furniture came from the workshops of Jacob-Desmalter. Behind Napoleon's *bureau mécanique*, similar to those in his other palaces, one can see the fine elm writing table used by his private secretary. The green corded silk that covers the seating is also used for the curtains, with their simple gold trimmings. Green is a colour often associated with libraries, studies and other workrooms, as it is reputed to be restful on the eyes.

Page 201: This clock, with a figure known as 'a woman reading on a couch', was designed in 1812; the example seen here, signed by the bronze-caster Claude Galle and the clockmaker Jean-Simon Bourdier, was presented by Josephine to Marie-Joseph Grand de Lanzac in 1813. It is shown surrounded by morocco-bound books from the imperial libraries.

Page 202: This magnificent flat-topped mahogany writing desk is enriched with gilt bronzes using many of the antique motifs so popular at the time, such as palmettes, griffins, and the thunderbolts of Jupiter. At each corner is a head of Hercules, inspired by an antique table which Percier had drawn in the Vatican Museum in Rome. We know that the model for casting was made by the sculptor Pierre Cartellier. The same figure of Hercules reappears, in gilded wood rather than bronze, on the throne which Jacob-Desmalter supplied in 1804 for Saint-Cloud.

Page 203: Almost every porcelain factory made inkwells, some with more success than others. The firm of Dagoty, which enjoyed the patronage of the Empress, showed great originality, as can be seen from this extraordinary piece of around 1805–10. This is an

inkstand rather than an inkwell: it includes an inkwell, a sander (holding powdered gum sandarac, to prevent ink smudging), and a pen holder. A putto in biscuit porcelain plays with an eagle with golden wings outstretched, perched on the truncated column of the inkwell, in green imitation bronze.

Pages 204–5: The roll-top desk continued to find favour with gentlemen, no less than fifteen being supplied to the palace at Fontainebleau during the Empire for the use of Napoleon's ministers. It was extremely practical, with different tiers and secret compartments for filing papers, and a top which could be rolled down in order to protect the contents from prying eyes.

THESE PAGES

Opposite: This bureau is mentioned in documents as having been supplied by the cabinetmaker Alexandre Maigret, but in fact it is the work of Charles-Joseph Lemarchand (1759–1826), whose stamp it bears. The gilt bronze motifs are similar to those found on two console tables by the same maker. It is quite an unusual design, as the flat top is surmounted by a mahogany cabinet flanked by terms with women's heads and feet in gilt bronze. The cabinet contains seven boxes covered in morocco decorated with a Greek key motif in gold.

Above: When the Empress Josephine died in 1814, the library at Malmaison

contained some 4,500 volumes, most of them bound in calfskin with the letters 'BP' intertwined on the spine, for 'Bona-Parte'. The books were auctioned off in 1929, but the museum of Malmaison has been gradually buying them back, and there are now around 600 volumes on display.

Lighting

Lighting was of course an important feature in all houses and apartments, and the available forms of lamp could vary quite considerably.

Torchères were the rarest because they were extremely expensive. They were generally made of gilt bronze or imitation porphyry, and their size – often more than 2 metres (6 ½ ft) high – enabled them to give more light than the smaller candelabra. The latter were often placed on console tables, close to mirrors so that the light would be reflected and hence doubled. Some candelabra, like those in the Throne Room at Fontainebleau, could hold up to thirteen candles. Sconces were always attached to the walls, and they too were reflected in mirrors; they usually had two or three branches, but could sometimes have up to seven.

In the main rooms of the apartment, there would always be a chandelier hanging from the ceiling, usually in gilt bronze and crystal. Chandeliers were also extremely expensive – one that held eighteen candles could cost more than 5,000 francs. For this reason, they were sometimes replaced by a *lampe à l'antique*, which had no crystal ornaments and was therefore less costly. In place of candles, there might be oil lamps known as Argand lamps, after their Swiss inventor, who was the first to feed a flame with a double current of air, increasing its brightness; the flame was protected by a cylindrical glass chimney, which improved the air flow and kept out draughts. These lamps were known in Paris as *quinquets*, after the pharmacist Antoine-Arnoult Quinquet, who – together with the distiller Lange – popularized them. Towards the end of the Empire period, a further improvement was introduced by the clockmaker Bertrand Carcel, who hit on the idea of pushing the oil upwards with a small pump powered by clockwork.

In addition to these forms of lighting, which were generally fixed, there were the traditional candlesticks of gilt bronze or silver-plated copper, which could easily be moved from one room to another, and the *flambeau couvert* – sometimes referred to as the *lampe bouillotte* – which for the most part was placed on a desk or table; its gentle light was tempered by a sheet metal lampshade, usually green, on a steel stem; the shade could be moved up and down the stem by adjusting a screw.

Although the use of oil lamps became increasingly widespread, candles of different types continued to be the principal light source during the Empire. The *chandelle* or tallow candle was generally made from beef or mutton fat and was less expensive than the *bougie* or beeswax candle, which took its name from the town of Bougie (Bejaïa) in Algeria, where it is said to have originated.

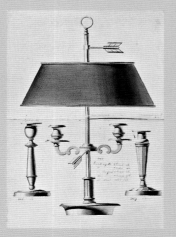

Left: A *flambeau couvert* flanked by two candlesticks, from a catalogue issued by the firm of Lancelot in 1806. In the apartments of the imperial residences, candlesticks might be made of gilt bronze, silver-plated copper or plain copper, depending on the rank of the occupant.

Opposite: *Man Reading by Candlelight*, 1814. This painting by the Danish artist Georg-Friedrich Kersting (1785–1847) shows a man reading by the light of a gilt bronze *flambeau couvert*. This type of lamp had between two and six candles under a single shade of painted sheet metal which could be raised or lowered by turning a screw. Such lamps were also known as *flambeaux de bureau* or *flambeaux de jeu* – the latter name because they were often used at gaming tables. They were also called *lampes bouillotte*, after a popular card game.

2894
30

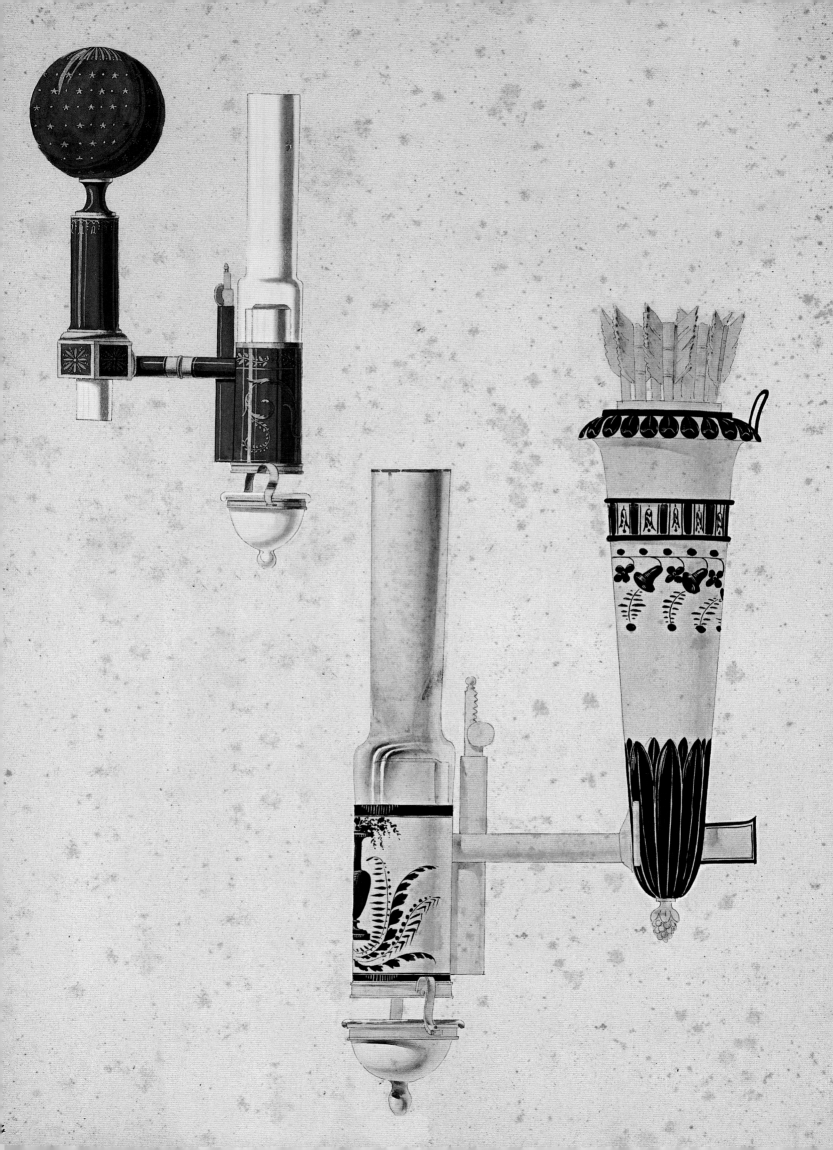

THESE PAGES
Left: This magnificent chandelier with sixteen branches was made for Josephine's boudoir at Saint-Cloud, probably by the bronze-caster Claude Galle, who provided most of the palace bronze work in 1802 and 1803. Its most remarkable feature is the relief decoration in the form of four chariots. The crystal – like that for most chandeliers of this kind – came from the Montcenis factory at Le Creusot, directed by Ladouèpe du Fougerais. The chandelier now hangs in the *salon de compagnie* at Malmaison.

Left, below: One of the sconces supplied in 1808 by Galle for the Emperor's bedroom in the palace of Compiègne.

Left, bottom: Percier designed this extraordinary chandelier, with its rich decorations of gilt bronze, for the home of 'Citizen C'. This was probably Bernard-François de Chauvelin, former Ambassador to England, whose house in the rue de la Victoire had been decorated by Percier and Fontaine – the house that Josephine had visited before deciding to commission the two architects to work at Malmaison.

Opposite: The size of chandeliers varied according to the size of the room where they were hung. The Empress's Third Salon at Compiègne has an impressive chandelier with thirty branches and a green corded silk rope trimmed with gold, matching the colour of the chairs. It was specially made for the room by Galle.

PREVIOUS PAGES
Page 210: An exceptional *flambeau couvert* with five candles, which Napoleon III placed in the council chamber at Malmaison. It is notable for the rich ornamentation of its cornucopia-shaped branches, its delicately ornamented bowl-shaped base, and the elegant shade, which is held in place by supports in the form of crossed bows.

Page 211: Four reproduction oil lamps with chimneys were made for the vestibule at Malmaison in 1992, based on a design dated 1811. Of painted sheet metal, with two lights each, they are like the ones that lit the room in 1814 at the time of Josephine's death.

Page 212: The Lancelot firm offered an extensive choice of lamps in a huge variety of shapes. These could be fixed to the wall, hung from the ceiling, or simply placed on an item of furniture. They were made of painted sheet metal and covered in a varnish that was both water- and heat-resistant.

Page 213: Argand lamps (known in France as *quinquets*), invented by the Geneva physicist Aimé Argand (1755–1803), provided improved combustion thanks to a double draught which enabled the burner to give off as much light as ten or twelve candles put together. A small glass bowl under the lamp collected the hot oil.

Pages 214–15: Lighting was vital in dining rooms, and the table always had a centrepiece with several gilt bronze candelabra. This pair at Malmaison – signed 'Thomire à Paris' – have in their upper section a dish to hold fruit or flowers. On the console tables at the back are two gilt bronze candelabra, which can be turned into single candlesticks by removing the four-branched attachment at the top.

Gardens

Under the Empire a general passion for the art of gardening was intensified by Josephine's devotion to it and by the Emperor's own tastes. In 1813, Josephine wrote to her son, Eugène: 'My garden, which is the most beautiful thing possible, is more frequented by the Parisians than my salon, for as I write, I am told there are at least thirty people walking in the garden.' Fain, Napoleon's private secretary, recalled: 'When the Emperor looked out of his windows and saw the chestnuts in the garden putting forth their first leaves, he longed to have more than one door on the ground floor to open, so that he could go out onto the lawn and walk down an avenue of green . . . His impatience was like that of a schoolboy.'

A basic distinction should be drawn between the *jardin* (literally, garden), which was essentially an urban feature, and the *parc* or park which was associated with a château or country house, although theorists like Thouin and Morel went so far as to divide gardens into twenty-five different types such as Chinese, English, *pastoral* and *sylvestre*. From the middle of the 18th century, the straight avenues of the classic French garden gradually gave way to what the 'anglo-chinois' style, in which, in accordance with the precept of Jean-Jacques Rousseau that 'nature plants nothing in a straight line', winding avenues led from one garden building or folly to another and from scenic view to scenic view. The idea was to create a world of illusion, where temples, tombs, columns, pyramids and obelisks were often squeezed into a rather small space, as in the Parc Monceau. This idea was already changing at the end of the 18th century, with the arrival of the landscape garden or *jardin irrégulier*, which became fashionable during the Empire. Here, the hand of man was lighter, making use of the natural landscape, with art merely embellishing the details. An abundance of water was always a prime feature, flowing gently between lawns, tumbling down in torrents through rocks, or forming a tranquil lake. The aim was to recover the spirit of the Arcadian gardens praised by Virgil and imagined by painters such as Poussin and Claude. Alexandre de Laborde, in his *Description des nouveaux jardins de la France et ses anciens châteaux* (1808), several times referred to painting: 'The aspect is noble, and recalls those beautiful backgrounds that Poussin often used in his paintings, culminating in a structure made by man'; and later: 'At Ermenonville, we discerned several different moods artfully brought together by thematic transitions: here the wild landscapes of Salvator [Rosa], and there the noble lines and varied settings of Claude.'

In town, however, everything was different: here the garden was chiefly a place for strolling in. In Paris, only three large gardens were open to the public: the Tuileries,

Left: *Cherries*, by Philibert-Louis Debucourt (1755–1832). This hand-coloured engraving, from *Modes et Manières du Jour*, is one of 52 plates published by La Mésangère in 1800–1801. The subtitle reads 'Coiffure of hair and pearls'.

Opposite: *Portrait of Monsieur d'Aucourt de Saint-Just*, c. 1800, by Louis-Léopold Boilly (1761–1845). The elegant pose, the fine boots, the close-fitting breeches, the dark morning coat and the immaculate cravat all seem ill-suited to the gardening work that he appears to be engaged in, with a pruning knife in his hand and a saw leaning against the chair.

the Luxembourg, and the Jardin des Plantes. The garden of the Palais Royal was given over mainly to commerce, while the Parc Monceau was too far from the centre to attract visitors. The Champs-Elysées and the Bois de Boulogne were regarded as rather unsafe areas.

The Emperor left his mark on the parks of the imperial palaces. At Saint-Cloud, where the public still had great freedom of access, he contented himself with a terracotta tower at the top of the hill called the Lantern of Demosthenes, which was a replica of the Choragic Monument of Lysicrates, the first building in Athens to use the Corinthian order. At Fontainebleau he added two new gardens to those designed by Le Nôtre: the one known as the Jardin de Diane was of particular interest to him, because it lay directly outside his ground-floor apartment and served as his own private sanctuary, while the old Jardin des Pins was transformed into an English garden with a winding stream, groves of exotic trees, and a pool marking the site of the legendary spring called the Fontaine-Belle-Eau, which gave the château its name. The changes were a great deal more substantial at Compiègne, and were made at the time when he was preparing to marry Marie Antoinette's great-niece, Marie-Louise. He took a very close personal interest in the work, declaring that 'The important thing is to connect the château as swiftly as possible with the forest, which is

the true garden and which provides all the pleasure of this residence.' The architect Berthault, nicknamed the 19th-century Le Nôtre, threw himself into the task at once: he transformed the terrace into a pleasantly gentle slope, constructed a trellised walkway, 1½ kilometres (1 mile) long and wide enough to allow two coaches to pass abreast, and most importantly of all, he extended the view from the château for 6 kilometres (4 miles), as far as the Beauxmonts. At Versailles, Napoleon bought back the areas of the estate that had been lost at the Revolution, but opted for a garden that would be relatively simple to maintain. The fall of the Empire prevented the project by which Napoleon had planned to transform Le Nôtre's gardens and which he described in his *Memoirs*: 'I had conceived a very strange idea, and had even had a plan sketched out for me. From those beautiful groves of trees I got rid of those nymphs in such dreadful taste, those ornaments *à la Turcaret*, and I replaced them with panoramas in masonry of all the capital cities we had entered in triumph and all the famous battles that had brought glory to our armed forces.'

But it was only the park at Malmaison that really deserved to be called a new creation. At the time when Josephine bought the estate in 1799, it covered an area of about 132 hectares (326 acres), including 25 hectares (62 acres) of parkland; when she died, fifteen years later, it

Previous pages: Auguste Garnerey (1785–1824) was born into a family of artists and specialized in painting landscapes and interiors with almost photographic precision. His most famous works are his twelve views of Malmaison, which he appears to have begun in 1812 but did not finish until 1823, when he presented them to Prince Eugène, then owner of the estate. Here he shows himself leaning against a tree and drawing, on the bank of an artificially winding stream.

Above left: The view from the house at Malmaison. Garnerey's painting gives an impression of the extensive vista that existed before 1877, when the estate was divided up. The Marly aqueduct, in the background, looks like a Roman monument, and plays the role of a garden *fabrique*.

Above: In 1807, along the road leading to Saint-Cucufa, Berthault restored an old reservoir of the stream at Malmaison, and embellished it with a statue of Neptune (somewhat optimistically attributed to Puget) and two rostral columns from the château of Richelieu in Poitou. In the background, Garnerey shows the carriages of the Empress's entourage.

Right: The large greenhouse was one of the main attractions at Malmaison. The Empress liked to show it off to her visitors, whom Garnerey depicts at the entrance to the building. In the centre is a basin fed by a fountain surmounted by the figure of a seated satyr. The glasshouses proper lay on either side of this entrance.

extended over 726 hectares (1,790 acres), of which 70 hectares (173 acres) comprised the enclosed park. As soon as she had the necessary means at her disposal, she devoted all her attention to the garden, with a view to everything being done in the English style. She would not allow any straight lines, and the idea of an avenue planted simply to lead from one place to another seemed to her like a horticultural deadly sin. Her projects entailed an infinite variety: she wanted to see little temples, bridges, tombs and rocks – all the things that Fontaine, her architect, considered to be the silliest aspects of the English garden. Four architects succeeded one another in five years before she finally found an artist who could understand her wishes: Berthault. Both a designer and a landscape gardener, he reshaped the park, added some *fabriques* or follies, and dug out an artificial stream with ornamental bridges, rocks and grottos. At Malmaison, Josephine was able to indulge her passion for the natural sciences, and she made her park into a living laboratory. Unusual animals, such as black swans and kangaroos,

roamed the grounds, and some of the land was turned into a nursery for the cultivation of exotic trees and shrubs, which she then sent out through France. Almost two hundred new plants, including purple magnolia, tree paeony, hibiscus, phlox, camellia and dahlia made their first appearance in France in the greenhouses at Malmaison. Josephine's gardens played a crucial role in acclimatizing these exotic plants to their new French surroundings. The imperial family also owned vast estates outside Paris – those of Joseph at Mortefontaine, Louis at Saint-Leu, Lucien at Plessis-Chamant, Caroline at Neuilly, and Pauline at Montgobert – but none could match the fame of Malmaison.

In Paris, all the great houses in the suburbs of Saint-Germain and Saint-Honoré had a garden, small or large. The informal style was generally preferred, comprising a broad lawn with irregular edges, surrounded by long winding avenues with artistically arranged clumps of trees. Examples of such gardens were those of Murat at the Élysée Palace, Prince Eugène in the rue de Lille, and King Louis in the rue Cerutti. Chateaubriand had scathing words to say about the fashion for gardens in confined spaces: when those who had been dispossessed at the Revolution returned, he wrote, 'there was no exile so poor that he did not squeeze the twists and turns of an English garden into the ten feet of earth or courtyard that he had recovered'.

Left: At the time of the Empress's death, the park of Malmaison and Bois-Préau was enclosed within walls and extended over 70 hectares (173 acres). Under the Second Empire it was reduced in size to 50 hectares (124 acres), and today it covers just 26 hectares (64 acres), including various plots and the estate of Bois-Préau, donated by Edward Tuck in 1926.

Above: Berthault built the Temple of Love on the banks of the winding 'rivière anglaise' at Malmaison in 1807, to replace an earlier temple which Josephine had presumably tired of. The new one incorporated six columns taken from various churches in Paris, which the architect Fontaine intended for the Louvre before the Empress commandeered them. Garnerey shows the temple in its setting, facing an artificial islet, with swans and luxuriant rhododendron bushes.

Left: A plate depicting *Pongamia glabra*, from *Le Jardin de la Malmaison*, a luxurious volume of 120 plates commissioned by the Empress and published in a limited edition of just two hundred copies in 1803–4. The text was written by the botanist Étienne-Pierre Ventenat, and the engravings were based on drawings by Pierre-Joseph Redouté, dubbed the 'Raphael of Flowers'.

Opposite: No one but Prud'hon could have captured so vividly the charms of the Empress Josephine. Painted between 1805 and 1809, this famous portrait shows her without any of the imperial pomp and circumstance, surrounded only by the flowers that she loved so much. Undoubtedly she has been idealized and rejuvenated by the artist, for the model herself had no illusions, declaring that the work was that of 'a friend rather than a painter'.

PREVIOUS PAGES
Pages 224–25: Near the large greenhouse at Malmaison, Berthault widened the winding river into a small lake, which was enjoyed by a flotilla of boats of various shapes and sizes (the largest could sail only on the lake at Saint-Cucufa). Garnerey shows one of these sailing trips, which were a traditional pastime at Malmaison.

Bibliography

Abrantès, Duchesse d', *Memoirs of the Duchess d'Abrantès*, New York: J. & J. Harper, 1832

A.G., *L'appréciation du mobilier*, Paris, 1821

Anonymous, *Quelques semaines à Paris*, date unknown

Austin-Montenay, F., *Saint-Cloud: Une vie de château*, Geneva and Paris: Mame, 1831–34

Blangini, F., *Souvenirs*, Paris: Charles Allardin, 1834

Benoît, J. (ed.), *Livres précieux du musée de Malmaison*, exhibition catalogue, Musée de Malmaison, Paris: RMN, 1992

Benoît, J., *Napoléon et Versailles*, exhibition catalogue, Musée de Versailles, Paris: RMN, 2005

Carlier, Y., et al., *Napoléon à Fontainebleau: Musée national du château de Fontainebleau*, Paris: RMN, 2003

Chevallier, B., *L'art de vivre au temps de Joséphine*, Paris: Flammarion, 1998

Chevallier, B., 'L'hôtel Bonaparte', *La Nouvelle Athènes: Haut lieu du Romantisme*, Paris: Action Artistique de la ville de Paris: 2001, pp. 55–57

Chevallier, B., *Malmaison, château et domaine des origines à 1904*, Paris: RMN, 1989

Chevallier, B., *Musée national des châteaux de Malmaison et Bois-Préau*, Paris: RMN, 2006

Chevallier, B. (ed.), *Style Empire*, Paris: Valmont Editeur, 2000

Coural, J., *Le Palais de l'Elysée: Histoire et décor*, Paris: Action Artistique de la ville de Paris, 1994

Coural, J., *Paris, Mobilier national: Soieries Empire*, Paris: RMN, 1980

Cueille, S., *Le domaine de Rambouillet*, Paris: Monum, Editions du Patrimoine, 2005

Dion-Tenenbaum, A., *L'orfèvre de Napoléon Martin-Guillaume Biennais*, Paris: RMN, 2003

Fauville, H., *La France de Bonaparte vue par les visiteurs anglais*, Aix-en-Provence: Edisud, 1989

Fontaine, P. F. L., *Journal. 1799–1853*, Paris: Ecole Nationale Supérieure des Beaux-Arts, Institut Français d'Architecture, Société de l'Histoire de l'Art Français, 1987

Forbes, J., *Letters from France written in the years 1803 and 1804*, London: J. White, 1806

Genlis, Comtesse de, *Manuel de la jeune femme*, Paris, 1829

Grandjean, S., *Inventaire après décès de l'impératrice Joséphine à Malmaison*, Paris: RMN, 1964

Grandjean, S., *Les Grands Orfèvres de Louis XIII à Charles X*, Paris: Hachette, 1965

Groër, L. de, *Decorative Arts in Europe, 1790–1850*, New York: Rizzoli, 1986

Hortense (Queen), *Mémoires*, 3 vols, Paris: Librairie Plon, 1927

Hoskins, L. (ed.), *The Papered Wall: The History, Patterns and Techniques of Wallpaper*, 2nd ed., London: Thames & Hudson, 2005

Juvigny, S. de (ed.), *Du coup d'Etat de Brumaire à la fin de l'Empire Napoléon Bonaparte à Saint-Cloud*, exhibition catalogue, Musée Municipal de Saint-Cloud, Paris: Imprimerie Blanchard, 1999

Kameke, C. von, *L'hôtel de Beauharnais*, Stuttgart: Deutsche Verlag Anstalt, 1968

Laborde, A. de, *Description des nouveaux jardins de la France et de ses anciens châteaux*, Paris: Imprimerie de Delance, 1808

La reine Hortense: Une femme artiste, exhibition catalogue, Musée de Malmaison, Paris: RMN, 1993

Las Cases, E. A. D., *Le Mémorial de Sainte-Hélène: Journal of the Private Life and Conversations of Napoleon*, London: Henry Colburn & Co., 1823

Lavallée, J., *Letters of a Mameluke, or a Moral and Critical Picture of the Manners of Paris*, London: John Murray, 1804

Ledoux-Lebard, D., *Le Grand Trianon, Meubles et objets d'art*, Paris: RMN, 1975

Ledoux-Lebard, D., *Le mobilier français du XIXe siècle*, Paris: Les Éditions de l'Amateur, 2000

Ledoux-Lebard, G., 'Un apogée du style consulaire La décoration et l'ameublement de l'hôtel de Madame Récamier', *L'Estampille L'Objet d'Art*, no. 278, March 1994, pp. 64–89

Moitte, Mme., *Journal*, Paris: Librairie Plon, 1932

Moulin, J. M., *Guide du musée national du château de Compiègne*, Paris: RMN, 1992

Nouvel, O., *Wallpapers of France 1800–1850*, London, Zwemmer, 1981

Nouvel-Kammerer, O., *French Scenic Wallpaper, 1790–1865*, Paris: Flammarion, 2001

Pariset, Mme, *Manuel de la maîtresse de maison*, Paris: Audot, 1822

Percier, C., and Fontaine, P. F. L., *Recueil de décorations intérieures*, Paris: Didot l'Aîné, 1812

Pinçon, J. M. and Gaube du Gers, O., *Odiot l'orfèvre*, Paris: Sous le Vent, 1990

Reichardt, J. F., *Vertraute Briefe aus Paris, geschrieben in den Jahren 1802 und 1803*, Hamburg, 1805

Rémusat, Mme de, *Mémoires*, 3 volumes, Paris: Calmann Lévy, 1893

Riffel, M., Rouart S., and Walter, M., *Toile de Jouy: Printed Textiles in the Classic French Style*, London: Thames & Hudson, 2003

Samoyault, J. P., *Guide du musée national du château de Fontainebleau*, Paris: RMN, 1991

Samoyault, J. P. and C., *Château de Fontainebleau Musée Napoléon Ier*, Paris: RMN, 1986

Samoyault, J. P. and C., *Un ameublement à la mode en 1802: Le mobilier du général Moreau*, exhibition catalogue, Musée de Fontainebleau, Paris: RMN, 1992

Versailles et les tables royales en Europe XVIIe–XIXe siècles, exhibition catalogue, Musée de Versailles, Paris: RMN, 1992

Opposite: Like many sovereigns, Josephine kept a menagerie which included a number of birds. In the vestibule at Malmaison she had eight large cages housing birds from America, Africa and Brazil, whose songs charmed her visitors. Her interest in zoology also led her to gather a collection of stuffed birds such as this cockatoo, of which she had several specimens.

Index

Picture credits

All of the photographs in this book were taken by Marc Walter. Most of them are previously unpublished, but some appeared in an earlier book by Bernard Chevallier (*Style Empire*, Paris: Valmont Editeur, 2000): this applies to the images of the Hôtel de Beauharnais, fabrics by Maison Prelle and Tassinari et Chatel, and wallpapers from the collection of the Union des Arts Décoratifs.

Other archive documents, paintings and engravings are taken from the sources listed below:

Bibliothèque Marmottan: pp. 161, 212, 213
Bibliothèque Thiers: pp. 143, 160, 176 (above), 197
D. Aaron Collection: pp. 63, 193
Lefuel Collection: p. 127 (above)
Musée Carnavalet, Département des Estampes: p. 218
Musée de Malmaison/RMN: pp. 220–21, 222, 223 (above), 224–25, 226 (above).
Musée des Arts Décoratifs, photo: Sully Jaulmes: pp. 8, 47, 142, 178, 216 (below)
Musée des Beaux-Arts, Rouen: p. 100
Musée des Beaux-Arts, Tours: p. 82
Musée Jean-Honoré Fragonard, photo: Claude Muzzin: p. 123
Museum Oskar Reinhart am Stadtgarten, Wintherthur: p. 209
Palais des Beaux-Arts, Lille/photo RMN © Philipp Bernard: p. 219
Private collection: pp. 86, 87 (above), 164, 168, 172, 176 (below), 208
Staatliche Kunsthalle Karlsruhe: pp. 10–11

Acknowledgments

Many thanks to Jean-Paul Bessière of the Réunion des Musées Nationaux, as well as the curators and directors of all the museums and houses that gave us permission to take photographs for this book.

Special thanks to the following: Emmanuel Starcky, Château de Compiègne; Amaury Lefébure, Château de Fontainebleau; Madame Monié, Hôtel Bourienne; Pierre Arizzoli-Clémentel, Château de Versailles; Dominique Fabre, Maison Tassinari.

Thanks also to Véronique Bruignac-La-Hougue, who kindly checked the captions in the Wallpaper chapter.

Translated from the French by David H. Wilson

First published in the United Kingdom in 2008 by
Thames & Hudson Ltd, 181A High Holborn, London WC1V 7QX

www.thamesandhudson.com

Original edition © 2008 Studio Chine, Paris
This edition © 2008 Thames & Hudson Ltd, London

British Library Cataloguing-in-Publication Data
A catalogue record for this book is available from the British Library

ISBN: 978-0-500-51440-5

Printed and bound in Hong Kong